Wheelchairs
Scooters
And
Sticks

TERRY REYNOLDS

Leavitt Peak Press

ISBN: 978-1-961017-93-1 (sc)
ISBN: 978-1-961017-94-8 (e)

Rev. date: 08/09/2023

CONTENTS

Introduction vii

Chapter 1 1

Chapter 2 13

Chapter 3 26

Chapter 4 48

Chapter 5 66

Chapter 6 73

Chapter 7 86

Chapter 8 The Need For Accessible Transport 95

Chapter 9 100

Chapter 10 And Finally 118

INTRODUCTION

Wheelchairs, scooters, and sticks all things to do with mobility and access. My involvement in working with disability was purely by accident, and profit was my motive which you will read about in the book. However, it went much further as I could see that the more access, the better it was for everyone not just the wheelchair user. The mother with a pram or pushchair, the blind or restricted vision, and of course, the biggest emerging market of older people. So if you could show businesses they could make more money by providing access, they would get more customers and everyone would benefit.

I have spent over forty-three years providing accessible transport and holidays; and to this day, find it difficult to understand some people's attitude toward disabled people, especially in business. I was the first to provide accessible coaches commercially in the UK; I remember being asked by another coach operator if we could supply a coach to accompany his on an outing to the coast, which we did. The next day, he contacted me and said that his client had rang him, and said not to send any of those disabled coaches again. I told him, it was not disabled it was accessible. Even if I had not been in this business, I would not have thought about my coach as they had.

Although things are a lot better now, integration is still a long way off, as you will read throughout the book. It is up to us all to look at a much wider aspect of access, as disability or a reduced mobility all need access. You will also read that tourism is the largest business in many countries; and the more access you have in transport and accommodation, the more people you will attract, and of course the money will follow. My aim is for more integration, and I am hoping to run some British history tours later where inclusion from overseas will achieve this and be the first for the UK. People now working in the tourist industry are starting to get more aware of what is needed in transport and hotels, as well as excursion venues. All these things will in the end add up to more inclusion in all things, not just holidays.

TERRY REYNOLDS

CHAPTER 1

The roar of the jets increased as the aircraft started to accelerate down the runway. I was off again on yet another holiday trip to Orlando; this was my forty-fourth. With me I have a group of twenty pax (passengers), seven of whom are wheelchair users, the rest of the group are clients who accompany them and also our staff of which one is my partner. We met eleven years ago when she applied to become a holiday helper; we now run the tours together whenever possible.

Long haul flights such as these go very quickly as it's the same procedure, drinks trolley first then dinner, then we have to get the on board aisle chair to get clients to the very small toilets, which can sometimes be quite a challenge.

I sit back into my seat and glance out of the window as we start to climb over the north of England. I feel tired as I have already been up six hours, and have a lot more work ahead as well as the long flight.

When you are younger, you always hear people saying that time goes quicker when you get older, and I have to say this seems to be true. I have been arranging and operating these holidays since 1980, and have lost count on how many I have done. It must be over 500 and every one of them is unique, but one thing is always common to them all, and that is the laughter from the characters and the things that happen.

There have been many changes since I started doing these on the whole for the best. Mainly, the attitude toward people with disabilities, it was so different all those years ago and it must have been very frustrating; and to a degree, I know what it was like as when I was ten years old. I had a bike accident and could not walk for a year. I was lucky I kept my left leg, but remember to this day, the plaster of Paris and those terrible crutches and going to the hospital three times a week for over three months for leg exercises. I sometime look back and now think that it was meant to happen, so I was aware of just what it was like all be it for a short period. Also, it gave me knowledge of what it was like to be an outpatient on NHS ambulances being picked up from home to the hospital and retuned later, sometime very much later, and from that experience I was able to alter it when my company was the first commercial company to provide this service in the early '90s.

I look around the aircraft, and my mind wonders back to how it all begun.

Back in 1971, I started my own business with one mini bus driving children to a special school in a London borough. Over the next few years, I had built up the business to six minibuses— all used on special schools. These schools were dealing with behaviour problems, not physical disability. I had built up a good relationship with the customer, and used to visit them a few times a month looking for more business.

I was there one day when the lady in charge was speaking on the phone quiet abruptly. When she had finished, she looked very concerned. One of her colleagues asked her what was wrong. She crossed her arms and said, 'Well, I don't know what we're going to do now.'

It turned out that there was a new special school. This one dealing with severely disabled children that was due to open in six months, and the phone call was from social services saying that they were not able to provide the transport needed. This was 1976, and it was only social services that had vehicles that could carry people in wheelchairs; there were no commercial operators at that time.

I asked what would happen if they could not get the transport. She told me that the school could not open, and if it did it would cause problems as to the timing of the school day. 'This is totally unacceptable,' she said.

I left her office not giving it a thought; wasn't my problem anyway. That afternoon, I was driving my school run and I had pulled up outside one of the children's houses when one of the social services vehicles stopped in front of me. They called these vehicles ramp ambulances; the driver got out and went to the back of the vehicle opening the door then pulling down a ramp which protruded from the back. The escort then pushed the person in their wheelchair onto the ramp, and the driver lowered this to the ground. I got out of my minibus and asked the driver how this worked. He was very informative, and I found this fascinating and not that difficult to use.

During the next few days, I made some enquiries about these vehicles and found out how long it would take to get them. Armed with this information, I called in to see the lady in the transport office in the council to ask how she was getting on with her problem. Nowhere was her answer, I said that I had been giving her problem some thought and asked her if I could help, she looked at me and said how would you be able to help? I said that I had done some research on these vehicles and would like to supply them. She looked at me with some amazement, what do you know about transporting wheelchairs, nothing I said but it doesn't look that difficult. Well how many wheelchairs can you get on a vehicle? She got me there I hadn't a clue, so I thought let's ask her a question, how many wheelchairs had you planned for. She looked at me again with some disbelief and went to a file on her desk, she flicked through this and said it looks like at least fifteen, and they will stay in their wheelchair whilst travelling. Are you really serious about this she said, very I said, could I ask you for the address so I can look at this and work out the route timings and costings.

To my astonishment, I left her office armed with all this information and a lot of work ahead of me. It couldn't be that hard, could it?

The next few days were spent on the phone, getting vehicle quotes, and delivery dates; I had taken the name of the lifts that were fitted on the social service vehicles so I knew where to get them, and they had told me of people who would fit them in the vehicles. The one thing I hadn't taken into consideration was how a wheelchair is secured in the vehicle so I had a look once again on how the other vehicle done this. To my surprise, it was just strapped to the side of the vehicle, two staples holding it to the side, but it seemed to work. When I took delivery of the first vehicle, I sat in a wheelchair that was strapped to the side; and someone tried to tip the chair with me in it, but it stayed secure.

I ended up with six of these vehicles, and we started the new school on time. This was to be just the start as more and more organisations found out about our accessible transport; I had by accident found a transport niche. I had not done this for any sort of compassionate reason. It was solely financial, it made money, and as I found out it was a very large market. As the business grew, I began to wonder why disabled people had been ignored for so many years; why weren't there services they could use, why was access such a big deal? To me, it seemed and still does very easy; and of course, access means the more easily you make it the more people will use it, and the more money you will make.

Over the next few years, the business started to grow very quickly. The reason being was no one else was doing it. For some reason, wheelchairs seemed to frighten people. I am sure they must have thought I was operating some sort of charity, as it was only them that dealt with disabled people; hardly anyone else in the commercial world did. When I used to speak to other coach operators, and indeed in later years' hoteliers, they used to say disabled people haven't got any money, and it is not commercially viable to pay for any adaption for the odd wheelchair customer that was to prove a great misconception on their part.

As well as operating school transport to then special schools, I started to get involved with private hire. This involved taking disabled people on outings to the coast ECT; this was usually from charity organizations that by using us could start doing it regularly. This was my first experience with adults as we had only been operating this transport for children. I ended up driving different people with different disabilities, which was a great education and was to prove invaluable years later. People's views on disability have changed since that time, and it seemed to me that they were isolated and stuck. I remember the first excursion I drove to Eastbourne from Hammersmith. I had told the passengers I would stop at the place I had always used when driving coaches for a coffee and toilet break. It never dawned on me that wheelchairs would not fit in the toilets, which of course they didn't. Although there was a one to one helper ratio, I had to give some help myself as it proved very difficult to get some of the men into the cubicles—I don't know how the women managed. Throughout the struggle of getting them out of their wheelchairs and onto the toilet and back again (which I had never done before), this great sense of humour of the situation came across to me from some, one said to me that being in a wheelchair would be more tolerable if you didn't need to piss and shit every day. That stop took one and a half hours, and there were only five wheelchairs and five helpers. We finally arrived in Eastbourne where I dropped them at the pier, and arranged a time to pick them up. I had five hours to kill so I thought I would walk back into town, have lunch, and maybe sit by the sea as it was one of those rare days when it was sunny and warm. I walked across the road to a fish and chip restaurant, and ordered lunch. I sat there waiting when two of my passengers (one in a wheelchair) tried to get into the restaurant, but there were three large steps to negotiate. I got up to help, as did a few other customers and we got him down; they asked if I wanted to join them so I did. We had a great discussion about access if you were a wheelchair user, a cliché now of course, but then not many people had any idea how restricting access was if it never affected you.

You start to look at things differently. While I was walking back to the coach, I found myself looking at kerbs thinking how would you cross the road on your own. There were no drop kerbs then, but I didn't know they were called drop kerbs then and not many people did.

We left Eastbourne to go back to Hammersmith after dropping off the passengers; and as I was driving back to the garage, I was reflecting on what a great day it had been, and that having vehicles like this was meant to happen so many more could enjoy a day out there needed to be more access. This was my new goal and I had no idea where this was to lead me.

'Wake up, come on they are coming round with the dinner,' said Marian.

The continuous roar of the jets came back into focus. I didn't realize I had been asleep that long. 'You will have to get the on board aisle chair.'

'Why?' I said.

'Because Albert wants to go to the toilet.'

I got up and asked one of the cabin crew if they would get the chair. I went over to Albert whom I have known for many years. Indeed, he was on the first holiday I ran in 1980.

'You do pick your time for going, Albert,' I said. 'Can't help it, son. You know what it's like,' 'Yes,' I thought. 'I know alright.'

Now, I have to give you some information on Albert so you can picture him in some of the situations he has got me into. He has polio and when I first met him, he got around using two sticks; and for distance, would use his wheelchair. He is very stiff and cannot open his legs so he has a job to sit on a chair without slipping off. So when he is in an aircraft seat, he gradually slips down the seat, which is very awkward for him when the meals are served as he gradually slips down until his chin is resting on the tray table. The only way to lift him back again is from behind, which is fine if it is one of our groups sitting in that seat behind. As you can imagine, this is rarely the case and you have to ask that person if they would move for a while, while you position Albert back into the seat. This is fine unless the flight is over eight hours, which will mean that person will have get out of their seat two times for the toilet, and at least five times to reposition him; by this time, they are getting just a bit pissed off.

The aisle chair arrived, and I got behind Albert so I could take his weight while he got his balance— Albert was able to stand with assistance, many of my clients could not. I assisted him to the aisle chair taking care that he did not catch his bottom on the arm rest at the end of the seat. Some of the seats have lift up arms, but this one didn't. It would of course be so much easier if all the seats had lift up arms, and it would alleviate the problem. Also, the check in staff don't seem to know where they are on the aircraft, which I have always thought was strange. When they do the check in, they put you in seats, which are not really suitable. Unfortunately, and with my thirty years' experience, the attitude is just get them on and away because once they have left here, they are not our problem. They become the problem of the aircraft crew, and this has happened many times. If the person cannot bear any weight, it would mean you would need two people to assist. One lifting from the rear, and one taking their feet as you would have to lift them over the chair's arm.

I arrived at the toilet with Albert—anyone that has flown will know just how small these are. Once again because Albert can weight bear and stand, I can get him into the toilet without a great effort. The problem is that once he is sitting down, he cannot lock the door, which means I have to stand outside stopping people trying to get in and use it, and he can take ages once he gets in there. I remember once, we were coming back from Orlando when Albert wanted to use the toilet I told him we were only forty-five minutes till landing but he said if he didn't go now, he would shit himself. I got the aisle chair, and got him into the toilet. Time started to pass a lot quicker than usual, which it does when you're busy, but Albert seemed to be in no hurry as the air steward kept asking if he was ready to come out and get back in his seat. In the end, the chief steward said that he had to get to his seat as they were coming into land. I opened the door of the toilet, and said he would have to get back. He said he could not as half was out, and he had another making its way out (he had a way with words did Albert). I said to the steward what he told me, and that I would have to physically pull him off the seat smelling like hell and sit him down next to a person not of our group in that condition, as he had no intention of moving voluntarily. The steward said that no one is allowed to land in the toilet. I can tell you history was made that day as Albert did. The landing was quite bumpy, which must have helped Albert with the second half as he soon come out after landing.

Albert was now back in his seat, and I in mine. It was time to see what was on the entertainment system. I sat back and started to think about the landing procedures in five hours' time listening to a radio comedy programme, which I thought was quite apt as getting on and off aircrafts is a comedy in itself. Anyone that can walk would not give a second thought to the getting on and off an aircraft, as I didn't, until—yes, when I took my first group.

* * *

Many things have changed since 1980 on airport and aircraft procedures mainly for the better, and of course so it should be. There is now an EU law on how people with reduced mobility (PRMs) have to be dealt with. It is now the responsibility of all EU airports to provide this service, and some do it better than others; and before the new law, it was the airline that provided the service and this could vary a lot.

My first holiday flight was back in 1981 with a small group to Miami with Laker Airways. There were no problems as the Laker staff were great, and it helped being a small group. The reason for going on this trip it was the international year for disabled people, and the new Disneyworld had not long been opened. Unfortunately, Epcot was still to open so at the time we could only visit the Magic Kingdom, but this was to be the start of round the world travel.

So how did holidays start from transporting disabled children to school and private day trips to the south coast from London? There was one person that through his determination and hard work to show that disability should not be a barrier, and that was Bill Hargreaves MBE who had been part of the then Spastics Society (now Scope), and had been one of the first people to arrange holidays for the residents in the society. I met Bill in 1979 because he had found out that we had accessible vehicles that he could hire, and wanted to see them and of course find out the cost. We met in his office at Fitzroy Square in London. It was also the place I found out later where his holidays departed from. Bill had cerebral palsy and used to have to swing his body at a certain speed to walk so he had a real problem walking slowly. I showed him the vehicle, and we then went to lunch in a pub that he knew. He asked what made me want to operate vehicles that could take wheelchairs, and where did I get the idea from. I told him about the special school problems, and that I could see a business opportunity because no one else was doing it. He looked at me, and said I was either naive or very brave jumping into the market like I had. I told him about the day trips that I had undertaken, and what I had found out about the lack of access. Bill said that things will only change when more and more disabled people travel, and that the people he took on holidays were pioneers that would change things over many years. Of course, he has turned out to be correct and that has happened. He said that my vehicles were just a start, but he needed large coaches that he could use on his holidays but would tell people in the society about ours anyway. The following week, he had a holiday leaving London going to Switzerland via Paris, and would I like to come down to see it off and why large coaches were needed. I agreed and would meet him early the following Saturday.

What I saw that Saturday was to direct me into the large accessible coaching business, and to promote access to as many coach operators as possible. I arrived at 07.30 to find the place full of people in wheelchairs—many had stayed overnight. Bill was also there with his wife, Mary, organizing the police cadets who he used to use as helpers. There were about fifteen wheelchair users plus twenty others including the ten police cadets. There was also a very large amount of luggage. I looked at all this and thought how the hell are they going to get this on the coach when it arrives. Many people were using the accessible toilet before the coach arrived as Bill was telling them there was to be a few hours before they got on the ferry. I look out of the door to see the coach and trailer pull up outside. The fun was about to begin. The cadets started to take out the luggage, which was loaded into the boot leaving the fifteen wheelchairs for the trailer. They then started to wheel out the chairs; then one cadet would lift under the arms, while the other lifted the legs as they struggled up the coach steps. It was so undignified especially for the women. I watched this with horror, and thought I can do something about this and I will.

9

The following week, I started to research how you would go about converting a full-sized coach. This was easier said than done in 1979 because guess what, there was no Internet. You had to use the telephone and contacts that you had. I found out about a charity that had one converted at Plaxton in Scarborough. I contacted them and went up to see how they did this, and how much it would cost. There were also technical issues that go with what was then the certificate of fitness. Plaxton told me that the certifying officer will issue an approved alteration certificate on completion. I worked out the costs and income as I had researched the possible private hire market, which turned out to be considerable. I had two second-hand coaches that would be sent to Plaxton for conversion, which would take three weeks. Bill Hargreaves was over the moon with the idea of accessible coaches for his holidays, and was letting everyone know including one of his close friends Joan Brander who was the founder of the wing fellowship trust—now renamed Vitalised.

The vehicles were ready on time and we took delivery. Under the regulations at the time, no one could travel on the coach in their wheelchair; they had to transfer to a seat. It was a start though as you could now enter and leave the coach using its newly fitted lift, not being hauled up the stairs as before. They later changed the regulations to allow the operator to take seats out of the coach to be able to leave people in their wheelchair. The department of transport recognized that vehicles had to be made more easily accessible so that more operators would do this, and I served on the policy transport committee in 1980 to look at access on public transport. In the end, they set up a permanent section dealing with access, which is still there to this day as well as all bus routes having accessible buses.

Bill used to visit my office in West London as he lived in Wembley —he would often come in before going to London. In his office, he had trusted staff that he had trained to administrate the holidays for the society. They would produce a brochure, which would then be sent to all the societies' centres, and at the time there were many of them. They in turn would apply for one of the holidays, filling in the detailed form about the care they required, and this was supplied by the police cadets assigned to the holiday. The amount of holidays run depended on the funds available as this had to come from the society so there was always a case where demand outstripped supply. This was leading Bill to try and keep the price of our coaches down to the same level as non-accessible coaches, and he was very good at negotiation. Our coaches would of course be more expensive due to the conversion costs, but of course with in reason. Both Bill and I worked on the following year's brochure, which would include one flying holiday; the rest would be by coach, some in Europe, the rest in the UK. We were also able to keep the hire cost down by using time slots where we knew there would be less private hire work. The brochure was printed and sent out to the centres, and bookings were coming in to Bills office. Then I received a phone call at home late at night from Bill there was a funding problem at the society, and all non-essential services had to be stopped; and of course, that included holidays.

The next day, I was in my office looking at ways to fill the gaps now available due to the cancelations. I thought, what a shame as it is going to cause such upset to the people looking forward to their holiday; and for many of them, it would have been their first. I spoke to Bill who was very upset, and all of the cancellations he would have to make. He said that he would be able to pay me a cancellation fee as he would other suppliers. Later that day, I was sitting at my desk looking at figures thinking how much the society was going to pay out on cancellation fees when a thought occurred to me. I rang Bill and he said, which always amazed both of us, 'Are you calling to say that you want to run the holidays?'

Bill invited me to his house for dinner that night to discuss and work out how this could be done. We looked at the figures. It was tight, but could be done for that year. Also, I would need someone experienced to assist, as this was all new to me. A meeting was set up with the director of the society to get their opinion, and explain how they would be run. The director at the time was someone called Tim Yeo, who of course went on into politics. Tim listened to our proposition, and looked at our figures. He looked up at me and said,

'Are you sure you want to do this? It's a great move forward for a commercial company.'

'Disabled people have to have more of a choice than they have at present,' I said. 'And who knows this could be a start, and I would also say you are brave in your decision if you let me go ahead.'

A few days later, they agreed with the proposition, but Bill was to become a consultant to us and we would pay something toward his costs. This was to be an arrangement that would last for many years, and help bring accessible holidays to the reach of many more people with many disabilities.

CHAPTER 2

It's very early in the morning, and I make my way to our garage. As I arrive, the driver Sam is attaching the trailer to the coach. This is to be it! The first holiday arranged by me with a lot of help from Bill. I have had to work out the timings, rooming, as well as everything that goes with running a holiday for disabled people on a commercial basis, but this has never been done before! Our pick-up is in London where we have forty-six passengers. They include ten police cadets that were arranged by the charity to act as helpers, thirty-four clients (all with cerebral palsy of which ten are wheelchairs), and Bill Hargreaves and his wife, Mary.

We arrived at the pick-up thirty minutes early. There was plenty of activity going on, and I don't think I have ever seen so much luggage in one place. Bill and Mary came over to the coach, and informed me that nearly everyone was here except four others that would be arriving in thirty minutes due to a mishap. Although we had a lift on the coach, as I have explained due to the regulations at the time, we could not transport people in their wheelchairs so we had to take them up on the side lift in their wheelchair then lift them out into the coach seat. By this time, of course we were quite expert at this due to the amount of private hire work we had done with many groups on day trips. All of my drivers had been trained by me, mainly on the job. There was no manual or school to go to as it hadn't been done before, but it has to start somewhere just like holidays.

We started the loading with the help of the cadets with the wheelchair transfers first. Although we were loading quickly, it seemed to be taking ages. We were then on our way to Dover for the ferry to Calais then onto Paris for overnight then onto Switzerland. As we were making our way to Dover, I would talk to the passengers telling them how long it should take to get to the dock and what will happen when we get there. On arrival at Dover, I had to make sure that when we were parked, we were by the lift to be able to get our wheelchair passengers off and up into the ferry.

Trying to get some of the people to understand why you needed the lift side clear was sometimes like asking for a bag of gold. They just did not understand they had not seen a coach with a wheelchair lift before, and the amount of times they tried to load us in the wrong place over the years was unbelievable. I asked Bill if he would go up with the passengers(pax) as they got off, which he did with eight of the cadets; while the driver, the other two cadets, and myself carried on unloading. By the time we had got all the passengers off the coach and into the ship, we had moved out of the harbour. I knew it would take some time to get the pax back down to the coach, and to load them on so I went to the purser's desk to ask if he would call the pax of my group to go down to the coach thirty minutes before we docked, which he did. (Could you imagine them doing that now?) I looked around and saw everyone working at the toilet—there were no access toilets then. By the time everyone had used the toilet and grabbed a sandwich, it was time to load the coach again. Once again, my driver and two of the cadets went down to the coach ready to start loading. Even though we were quicker loading, it still took some time and we're constantly being asked by the ferry staff how long we would be as they had an empty ferry that needed loading.

We left the ferry, and stopped at the customs and passport control.

The passport control asked me if all the passengers were British, I said they were. He then asked me to tell them to get off the coach, and go through passport control. I said it could take some time as ten were in wheelchairs. I am sure they did not believe me as he come out and got on the coach. He then believed me, and asked a few of his mates to come and have a look. They had not seen this before, but this was just the start of many, and you don't realize this at the time. The journey to Paris was about three to four hours without a stop, and that was the plan; but of course that never happened. What you learn when coach driving is that the most you can sometimes get away with, without a toilet stop, is two to three hours. Of course, it is worse when you get off a ferry that has so much drink on board; hence, toilets are needed even sooner, and yes they were. Now we are in France and I do not speak French and I have to find a place that has some larger toilets, and explained to them it could take some time. Sure enough, two hours later there were requests for toilets. I told the driver to stop at the next service area. Now in 1980, in many service areas in France, the toilets were in the shop or restaurant area so when we pulled up outside the shop, we then had to get the ten wheelchairs from the trailer and start getting the clients into them. As you can imagine, this does take some time. Whilst this was going on, others that did not need the lift were leaving the coach and heading toward the few toilets there were. Of course, unlike the UK, you have to pay to use the toilet in France, but we will come back to that later.

There seem to be a problem as one client had been put into the wrong wheelchair, and he wasn't happy. The police cadet concerned said he didn't know whose was whose; they had no name on them. 'I just took the first one from the trailer. It's only to get him to the toilet and back. Does it really matter?'

I must admit for a while I was agreeing with him until Bill came over to see what was going on. I told him and he looked at me and said, 'Well, you may know about transport, but not about wheelchair users. These are their legs,' he said. 'They mean a lot to them. They don't want other people sitting in them, especially going to the toilet and back.'

You see, until you are involved, you don't think of that. Of course they want their own wheelchair, it is important. We found the right wheelchair and changed it. Then we labelled the other nine, and from that day, loaded them in order. We started to take the wheelchair users into the shop where the toilets were. As was the usual, the doors were too narrow to take a wheelchair into. We had to park the chair and where they were women, two of the girl cadets would try to lift the client from the chair for them to get their balance then very slowly into the toilet where, whilst standing, trousers and knickers down then onto the toilet seat. All of the time any other woman from the public walking past as they entered and left the toilet block. I remember thinking this really can't be right. Wheelchair users have been around for years, why hasn't someone done something? I remember asking Bill this question later, and he told me that when wheelchair users start travelling and get a bigger voice, people will realize like yourself that here is a market; and when that happens, things will change. And he looked at me and said, 'I am sure you will let people know more loudly than many others.'

He was right of course, and over the years with markets adapting and legislation, things have changed and one-day access will be for all. We continued with the toilets, which took over one and a half hours; and by the time we had got them back on the coach and got ready to go, it was two and a half hours. I used to write all this information down so I could use it when I later used to plan excursions and holidays. I found it very handy, and used to think to myself one day I will plan a coach holiday and it would all go to time; and later it did, and found that the information I was now gathering would be invaluable later.

We arrived at our hotel just outside Paris three hours late. Indeed, we had to go straight in for dinner; easier said than done because yes you are right, we had to do the toilets first. I went into the restaurant to make sure the correct amounts of tables were there. The head waiter came over and asked where the group was. I told him, but he didn't understand why it was taking so long, I think he started to understand as they come in. Bill and I were trying to arrange the seating as some of the clients needed help with their food Of course, the restaurant had no understanding of the amount of room we would need as a wheelchair takes up more room than a standard chair. Therefore, a table for six could only manage four. Well, I can tell you French waiters don't like their restaurants altered as we tried to get more tables, taking up more room than what was planned for us. In the end, they had to separate some of us causing great disruption. Once this had been done, they then started to bring out the dinner.

There was an English woman near my table, and she was having a moan about her meat saying it was too undercooked. The problem was she was quite loud about it as I think she was being ignored. The problem was that the more ignored she was, the louder she got; and in the end, picked up her plate and walked into the kitchen. Big mistake! You don't do that in France in a French kitchen. There were loud voices followed by a crash of crockery then a scream as the lady was chased out of the kitchen by a chef wielding a chopper. Both were captured by other hotel staff, and taken out of sight. The manager then came in and apologized in French then in English,

I was talking to a number of clients about their life, and asked what they had seen and experienced and how did they like the coach. All said it made the boarding a lot easier, but some would have liked to have stayed in their wheelchairs. I told them that at the time, I was on the policy committee at the Department of Transport, and I had put this high on their agenda. The problem with the committee was that most were civil servants, and none of them had seen how hard it was lifting people in and out of their wheelchairs. This would change in the future. I really enjoyed my talk with the clients that night, and as the drinks flows, the subjects we started talking about you wouldn't believe; but of course if you didn't have a disability I would say that, wouldn't I?

I am sure I had a slight hangover the next day as we got clients down for breakfast, and whilst that was going on, we were loading the luggage. We were aiming for a 9 a.m. leave, but that got to 10.10 (I will get this on time by the end of the holiday). We joined the motorway system, which unlike the UK, we had to pay for; and it is only just recently they now pay to use our roads. Now that we had done toilets a few times and got to know the clients by name, I had worked out the best place for them to sit to make the loading and unloading of the coach quicker. Of course, if we had been allowed to keep them in their wheelchairs; but hey, we had travelled for two and a half hours so I knew I would have to stop soon. I went to the front of the coach to the courier seat next to my driver, Sam. This was Sam's first time abroad driving a coach—I am sure he was finding the experience interesting. I asked him how many km (kilometres) to the next service area, he said thirty, and I told him to go into that one. I stayed at the front talking to Sam, and looking at my map books and drawn route. Apart from Bill and Mary and a couple of clients, none of us had ever been to this hotel. Indeed, neither Sam nor myself had been to Switzerland before so this was going to be very interesting.

We soon pulled into the services, and to my amazement, it all went very smoothly. We were in and out in less than one hour. We were getting used to the clients, and the team were getting used to the coach and me. We later stopped for lunch, and I told Sam to go off so he could have a break without getting interrupted. As a coach driver myself, being away from the passengers is a break you need if you have many more hours ahead, which he had. We were soon on our way to the Swiss border, and already we had noticed the scenery was getting better. We went through the French border, and stopped at the Swiss. I went over to the window, and he asked me if they were all British. I told them, yes. He said to ask them to get off and go through here, pointing to another doorway. I told him that could take some time and explained ten were in wheelchairs (roll stalls), I had learnt the German word. He looked at me with some amazement as he couldn't see the wheelchairs. I explained and showed him where they were. He comes out of his office and got on the coach looking down the aisle. I told everyone to hold up their passports, which they did as he walked down the aisle checking some. He asked where I was going, I told him, 'Einsie deln'.

'Oh, good,' he said. I thought that was a very strange thing to say; later I realized why.

The scenery was becoming breath-taking. I was very impressed with this country, and was looking forward to doing the excursions.

We were now picking up the signs for Einsiedeln, and the clients were getting excited (or they just wanted the toilet).

What I was about to find out was that Einsiedeln was a pilgrim town where people came who had a disability to be cured, hence, the comments from the border staff. It was built around a huge monastery at the top of a hill. It was totally self-sufficient as it had cattle, as well as huge gardens where they grew what they needed. Our hotel was just below it, and had been used by Bill and the society on numerous occasions. We pulled up outside on the left hand side of the road so we were pointing toward the traffic coming toward us, which as you can imagine, started to cause a lot of congestion, and it wasn't long before the local police arrived. Lucky enough, the manager of the hotel who knew Bill came out and spoke to the police as they didn't speak a word of English. As Bill knew the hotel and had a rooming list, it was agreed that he and a couple of cadets would take the people in and get them to their rooms. We unloaded the trailer of its wheelchairs, and started to get the cases from the boot—as you can imagine, there were a lot of it. As we sent the wheelchairs up on the lift, I just happened to look around; and to my amazement, there were at least thirty odd people watching as clients were put into their wheelchairs and bought down on the coach lift. Even though this was a sort of pilgrim town, people had never seen wheelchair clients transported this way before. Not only were they watching, many were also taking pictures, and over the next week this would happen all the time.

The last client was now off the coach. I went inside, and checked to see if anything had been left on the shelves or seats. I didn't see anything, and told the driver to park up the coach and I would see him back in the hotel. Now this hotel was booked by the then Spastic Society who wanted to provide holidays to their beneficiaries, and was organized by Bill. Bill wasn't a tour operator, and at the time neither was I; Bill had a walking disability, and truly believed that disability should not be viewed or treated by others as it was. Disabled people should be able to travel and enjoy holidays, family life, and a job. Indeed, for many years, that was Bill's job; going around many companies around the country trying to convince employers that with a few adaptions, this could happen. Of course, he was absolutely correct and has since been proved right, and he did live long enough to see most of it happen. I told you this because when I walked inside the hotel, it was absolute chaos. One of the reasons was that, although it was a hotel of sorts, the front was a cafe/restaurant; and as you went in, the lift was immediately on the left. I say lift but… I have seen many lifts in my time, but this was small and the cadets were having a job to get them in. Also, there was no inner door so you had to be careful as you could get scraped against the wall as the lift went up. Getting the ten wheelchairs up took a long time, and of course that was just the start. We then had to sort the room out.

With the help of Bill, I went round the rooms to see if the cadets were coping, which all in all they were. Bill was showing how to arrange the room, and that by teaming up, they would manage a lot easier. We arranged a time for dinner with the hotel and the clients. I said to Bill I was going downstairs to have a beer or two; he joined me later. I asked him why he had chosen this hotel, as it was not easy. He told me that he used a travel company that provided both the coach company and hotels. He told me that he had told the company that the hotel was not ideal, but they had told him it was very difficult to find a hotel that would take that amount of wheelchairs. Indeed, it was difficult to find any hotel that would take any wheelchairs, which I would find out in the next few years. Both Bill and I had worked out the excursions, and he had told me that the cable car he had used before could take a wheelchair, as could the boat on Lake Luzern. Now, all we had to do was work out the timings. As you can imagine, there are many things to take into consideration when working out these timings. We need to know what time the hotel wants us back for dinner then we would allow two hours before this to get back to allow for getting ready; and because I knew approximately how long it would take to get to the cable car, I could work out our leaving time.

At dinner that night, I went around all our tables to ask people what they thought of the holiday so far. Many thought that they were still run by the society, and that I just run the coach—they were surprised but were very pleased with the coach. I told them that tomorrow was a free day to get to know the town, and of course, the cathedral where miracles happen. Indeed, inside, there are many pairs of crutches hanging on the wall. I enjoyed the rest of the evening getting to know the clients, having a drink with them, and learning about their lives and problems they had had to face coping with their disabilities—these were an eye opener. It made me realize how many wheelchair users there were and that not many things had ever been done to make their lives easier and more accessible.

The next day after breakfast, most people went over to the cathedral and others explored the town, which was full of little shops and of course large gift shops. I was in my room and had put in a call to my office (no mobile phone then). Before I had left to run this holiday, we had contacted many charities to see if they wanted to do any excursions using our other accessible coach; and the news was we had sold out of dates, and could have sold many more if we had more coaches. There was a market here, which had been ignored for years. I met up with Bill for a coffee, and we started talking about this market. This is what I called it Bill didn't, but he understood that by showing it as a market, the commercial world might get interested, and it could be the way of changing things. I asked Bill why were things, in my opinion, so bad for disabled people. Simple things like drop kerbs would make getting around in a wheelchair so much easier. Bill said most people were unaware of what was needed.

'Like yourself,' he said. 'It's only since you have come into this so called market you are aware of the problems. The more people like you that come into it, the more it will change.'

And I thought how right he is. You really do start to look at all things differently, and you hear that there are millions of disabled people and nearly all at present have to get out of their wheelchair to travel, I thought. We have had men on the moon, yet you have to get out of your wheelchair to travel. There is something really wrong.

The following day was a trip on the boat from a town on the lake where we would board the boat, and a two-hour cruise into Luzern where the coach would pick us up. Bill who had been on the boat a few times said that chairs could go around the boat, and also could get into the cafe/restaurant on board. The Swiss being the Swiss have to be on time, so as we got the wheelchairs off the coach, they were taken to queue up where the boat would dock. The boat came into dock, and the passengers getting off were quickly shown the way. Once off, just like clockwork, our clients were taken by the crew and pushed up a ramp onto the boat where they were taken by our cadets and positioned for the best view. Within minutes, the boat was off and the views of the shoreline were fantastic. I went round to see if the clients were okay, and they all seemed very happy. I went into the cafe with Bill and Mary for a well-earned coffee and cake. Bill seemed very happy, and said he was so pleased with the holiday so far.

Mary looked at me and said, 'There is no comparison, the whole thing was better and the coach was the cream on the cake.' Then she looked at me and said, 'But you have a gift for this work, and I am so pleased you and Bill found each other.'

Whilst we were in the cafe, many of the cadets were coming in to get refreshments for the clients, as well as some bringing in clients for something to eat. Everyone had a great time on the boat, and it wasn't too long before we were pulling in to the city of Luzern. I had asked the cadets to wait together so others could get off the boat first as this was the safe way to exit. Once we were all off, we made our way to the coach park where I hoped I would find Sam and my coach. Until you see the group in a line, you really get a shock when you see how long it is. Ten wheelchairs and thirty-seven others take up a lot of room on a pavement, and they are all my responsibility. I am glad to say, yes, both Sam and the coach were waiting for us; we loaded the coach and went back to the hotel the scenic way, which Sam had worked out the previous night.

Whilst we were travelling back to the hotel, I noticed that a few of the cadets were fast asleep so I thought it would be a good idea to have chat with them to see how they were coping. Once we had unloaded, I asked the two who were earlier sleeping if they could join me for a drink, and ask another cadet to keep an eye on their two clients. The two who joined me were a nice couple of young men. We talked for the first few minutes about what they wanted to achieve in the police force. I then asked how they were getting on with the clients, they said not bad. I asked what they meant, they said it was very hard work, and how small the rooms were made everything very difficult including the lift to get up. They said they had never done anything like this before. I then shocked them both, and told them neither had I. They were looking at me with some disbelief. I put my arms in the air and said, 'Really.' I said what has Bill told you, they told me he had a word with the clients and told them about us, and that it was part of our training going on this holiday.

'The clients are fine,' they said. 'It's just that, we want to make sure we are doing things right.'

I told them not to worry and if they wanted help at any time, to find me or Bill. Just that little bit of time with them made all the difference, and as the holiday proceeded, I made a point of seeing all the cadets often.

Today was going to be an eventful day. Bill had told me about this excursion, which was a trip on a cable car; and since he first told me, I was trying to work out how this was going to be achieved without taking clients from their wheelchair. Bill assured me that no one had to leave their chair, but I was still apprehensive. We loaded the coach, and started to make our way to the cable car; this was worth it just for the fantastic scenery. When we arrived, a cable car was making its way up and passed over the coach—it was much larger than I had thought and now could see how clients could be kept in their chairs. The coach was soon outside the entrance, and I went off to sort out the tickets, whilst the coach was being unloaded. Things were getting better as I didn't have to say anything to the cadets as they knew what to do—dare I say it was working like clockwork.

Whilst the staff in the station were sorting out the tickets, I looked around to see how people got on and off the cable car. There was a platform, like at a train station, where the entrance was level with the floor; this enabled the wheelchair to go on, and parked next to each other in a line. Of course, there were no tie downs; they were many years away yet. As they were loaded, I asked each cadet to stand behind a wheelchair to steady them as we went up. It didn't take long before we were all on, and the doors were shut. Then, in a minute or so, there was a shudder as the cable car started to move; and as it did, so began to tip slightly, which as I could see did frighten a few including myself as this was my first time—mind you I didn't tell anyone.

As we proceeded up, the views got better and better. For the clients that could not take their own photographs, I announced that our staff would do it for them as this was something not to be missed. As we were nearing the top, I began to think about how accessible this place would be as it was a winter ski lodge. The cable car came to a rest at the platform, and the doors were opened. There were staff waiting to help us off, and this was done with the famous Swiss efficiency. We were guided to a restaurant with just fantastic views, and it was all very accessible. People started to have hot drinks and snacks, and all you could hear was the clicking of cameras and laughter. I went around the tables getting people's opinions, and they were just gobsmacked. One said to me that they never ever thought they would be able to do this without lots of effort, and said that with people like me, about anything will now be possible. I am not an emotional person, but as this person held my hand and looked into my eyes, I really did have a job to keep the tears back. I explained to her that I surely have a different motive to what she thinks as I was doing this for money. She said, 'Maybe, but it has started now because of you, now we will be able to travel the world like any other person.'

We got back to the hotel about 5 p.m. where people either had a rest or went out around Einsiedeln. I was in my room speaking to our office and working on some costing, and of course getting ready for the journey back. I had made some notes on where not to go in the future, and of course were to go, and to research other locations; but we had to do this one again even if it was just for the views. I went downstairs to the cafe where some of our clients were, and I got this real sense of happiness it was hard to explain. Clients kept asking me if I wanted a drink, and I would thank them and say maybe later. In all my life I had never felt like this, as in business you are rarely treated like this. I told Bill about how I felt, and he smiled and said, 'I knew you could do this,' he said. 'You have a unique gift of knowing what people want and going out of your way to make sure they get it. Just carry on like this and you will make things better, and unlike a charity, will be able to put over a commercial view to other commercial concerns.'

It was a long day, but at last we were back outside Fitzroy Square in London. As we pulled up, there were many people waiting to collect the passengers, they came from all over the country and others that were staying at Fitzroy. We started to unload. I was saying my goodbyes to the clients as the driver and cadets were sorting out luggage. Although you say it many times, I was still asking the driver to check the luggage racks just in case anything was left. Soon, everyone and their luggage were off the coach, and we were all saying our final goodbye. I had arranged for another driver to pick Bill, Mary, and myself up separately as the coach had to go back to our garage to get ready for a day job the next day; not with Sam driving though, a rest was due to him.

On our way back to Bills house, he said how pleased he was and that he looked forward to helping make a programme for next year. He would also be on a few more this year, but the pattern had been made for the future. After Bill and Mary had got home, I sat in the back of the car thinking about the holiday, and all the funny things that had happened. I thought you couldn't make this up, and started to tell my driver and he was also in fits of laughter. The driver dropped me home where I relived the holiday once more.

CHAPTER 3

My business was taking off and getting very busy. We now offered escorted holidays to all types of disability not just CP. We also offered three different care systems. Basic care where a client needed no personal help; Share Care where the client needed some help, and shared a helper with another client; and Exclusive Care where the client had their own helper supplied by us. We had found that in the early years, many potential clients did not know anyone they could take away on holiday; hence, they would not have been able to go. At this time, I only had experience in taking CP clients on holiday, and although I had met other disabilities on day trips, they were all grouped together with the same disability when they travelled. So I had no idea how they would interact with each other in a holiday situation. We all have to remember that this had never been done before on a commercial basis, and I remember talking to a large tour operator about maybe in the future they might be able to offer FIT (fully inclusive tours) to disabled people. There was a look of sheer horror on his face then that turned to laughter. 'You must be joking,' he said.

Why would we want to do that, and I am sorry to say you must be mad even thinking about it. Just leave it to the charities; that's what they are there for. I wouldn't want them on my holiday. I had come across this attitude many times when trying to make bookings with hotels, both in this country and abroad. It's the numbers game—to keep the price reasonable, you must have a certain number of people travelling. At the time when you said ten wheelchairs, there would be a silence and an abrupt *no* or they would go into one and say such terrible things like we are a good quality hotel, and I am afraid we don't take cripples. That was pretty general—and I mean worldwide. It was how it was then, it had to change; and if we could show that there was money in this market, it would start to be viewed differently, but that was a long way off at this time.

We started making our first company brochure, and wrote down a list of destinations by road and by air. We soon found out that in Europe, there were no accessible coaches for private hire so we knew it would have to be our coaches. As with the UK mainland, Europe was dependent on charities to supply service for disabled people. The brochure that was being planned was for 1981, which had been designated international year of disabled people by the United Nations. I had been asked by the then British Tourist Authority if they could use one of my coaches to carry some people from overseas around the country. Maybe at last something is happening. What I was pleased about is that I met some very interesting people who were also involved with accessible travel from other countries. I was also given an award for providing outstanding facilities to overseas disabled visitors, which was presented to me by Leonard Cheshire, and this still has pride of place in my office. Even to this day, I meet people who work for the Leonard Cheshire foundation but of course have never met him and now never will which makes my meeting with him even more special.

I had to plan this brochure on top of the day to day running of the company, which was getting busier everyday as we were getting known. I also had to price all the enquiries for coach hire and charter. It was then that I decided to promote one of my drivers who knew the day to day running as good as myself. That took a lot of pressure from me, and gave me the time I needed to get the holidays planned. Although I had the benefit of Bill's experience, I was now embarking on a new method of holidays as these would be open to all not a specific disability looked after by that charity. It was going to be interesting seeing how the charities would react. I wrote to the charities I found operating their own holidays to ask them if any of their beneficiaries might consider going with us. I never got a resounding no, but I could tell they were not that interested. I laid out a list of destinations, most of them by coach, a few by air, which went to Jersey. I had never done a brochure before, so a trip to the travel agents was called for. We decided that a page per holiday should do the trick, also a full page on our company, and of course our accessible coaches. Our customer base at that time was the spastic's society's holiday list, which Bill had. That plus a few hundred we should get through advertising.

Six weeks later, we received the first Chalfont Line brochure. We called in some drivers to help put stamps on the envelopes. We were lucky at the time as our office was right next door to— yes you've guessed it—the post office. All we could do now was wait.

The first results were not encouraging. Plenty of phone calls though, but it was the case that you now had to pay for care where it was included usually with the charity. Also at the time, it was before Motability so the only vehicle available for wheelchair users were the three wheelers, which were not the safest. With the introduction of mobility allowance, it made money available for use on leisure. As I have stated, there were many phone calls—mainly from people who were not part of the then spastics society—asking how the holidays were run, and what experience we had. We were able to answer most of their questions, but they really did like the idea of using an accessible coach, 'That will be heaven,' one of the clients said.

We also had another result due to my attendance at the department of transports policy committee. It was agreed that we could take seats out for clients to stay in their wheelchairs, so now we could have six static wheelchairs and thirty-two seated. This would make a big difference for some of the clients I had seen, and would make the whole holiday experience so much better. We are now ready to take people on holidays of a lifetime—or at least something different. These were the first escorted holidays now run on a commercial basis with a mixture of all types of disability. All having different needs going around the world. People were going to see things they thought they would never have seen in their lifetime, and it was about to begin.

It was the first long haul flight; it was booked with BA from Gatwick to Orlando. I had spoken to a nice lady at groups, who I was to know for many years before BA outsourced their group department. Arrangements were made for me to see the aircraft after it had landed, so I had to go to Gatwick quite early to meet with someone from BA. Once there, we met up, and I was taken to the gate where the aircraft would unload—could you imagine this being done now? The man from BA thought we were some sort of charity as they had never done this amount for a commercial company. He thought it was a great Idea and asked if I had been to Orlando before and what a fantastic place it was. This was my second time as I was there in 1981. Disneyworld was growing, and now Epcot was open. Everything in Orlando was new and exciting. We had nothing like it here in the UK; also because it was new, it was great for wheelchairs.

There was activity happening round the pier. The plane had landed and was on its way to the pier. The controller in charge asked me if I had ever seen a plane arrive from a long haul flight before, I said no. He said, imagine it has been in the air for over eight hours where people have been eating, sleeping, and farting, there will be quite a niff when the door opens; and of course, he was right. You see, it's something you don't really think about, as we get on after it's cleaned and freshened up. I asked if we could keep the wheelchairs to the gate, he said we could. He showed me how they would be taken down the stairs to the aircraft hold. That would happen after we transfer the passengers on to the aisle chair to take them to their seat. The aisle chair is what it says, and fits between the seats down the aisle of the aircraft. I was offered a go, so I sat on the chair and was taken backwards down the aisle. It worked well provided you were not too big. We then left the pier, and headed to the check in desks. There I met the check in supervisor, and we went through what would happen next week. I left Gatwick feeling confident, and drove back to Perivale.

The alarm went off. It was 4 a.m. I had a quiet shower so as not to wake my young boy, and drank a few cups of tea downstairs. I was waiting for one of my drivers to take me to Gatwick. I heard her pull up outside, and opened the door. She put my case in the back of her car, and I made sure I had all my papers, airline tickets, etc. We arrived at Gatwick at 6 a.m., and I saw one of my male helpers Denis there. He said that he had looked around, but hadn't seen anyone. Denis was good like that. He was always early and you could trust him. Over the years that I knew him, he was to do over 100 tours until his sad death in 2008.

We wanted to start the check in at seven o'clock as the flight took off at eleven. I had eleven wheelchairs in a group of thirty-eight. Soon, clients were arriving with their carers We had about four who were using ours as they had no one to go with them. They were all on exclusive one to one care. Denis told me that the other three helpers had arrived, and were having a coffee—Denis was of course the fourth helper. The coffee shop was starting to fill up with our clients, and looking quite full. I went around finding out who they were, and checking them off my list. I walked over to the check in where I met the person I had seen the week before. She looked up and greeted me asking if they were all here, I said about only half at present. She said it would be easier if we did the check in when they had all arrived as we could have our own check in desk. I walked over to the café, and started talking to the people there. We started talking about holidays and the ones they had been on, and how they were looking forward to this holiday. I told them what they were about to see, and where they would be staying. There really was an air of excitement amongst the group now.

Denis came over and said everyone was here so we could start the check in. I went over first and waited until two staff came over to the desk. I went over with all of the paperwork (there was a lot of it then), I looked round and everyone was lined up. I thought, my God I couldn't believe how many there were. Starting at the front, I started getting their names, and went to the desk with the luggage—this was a time before the regs we have now so it was a lot quicker. When they received their tickets, I told them to go through to the departure and duty free and the area they should then wait in. Denis went through with them to show them where to wait. The check in seemed to take forever, but of course there were a lot of people and luggage. I thanked the check in staff, and walked through security with the last of the clients. They went off to get their duty free, and have a drink so I showed them where to meet us later.

There are times at an airport (especially now), when you think you are walking to your destination as the aircraft gets further and further away from the terminal. I look behind me and it looks like a wagon train. We finally arrive at the gate, which was filling up quickly. They took us into the waiting area. 'How many can walk to their seat?'

'Only one of the wheelchair users' I said. 'All the rest could walk; all be it at a slow pace.'

In a jumbo jet 747, the seats are 343. This gives four aisle seats where I can put our staff and walkers. That means it is easy for them to get up and help with toilets ECT. Putting someone with limited mobility in an aisle seat is not the best thing to do, as they will then block others who can walk getting out. The people from special service (as it was then) arrived, and wanted to know who was sitting where. As I knew all of the seat numbers, I had planned who would sit where—it did not matter whose name was on the boarding pass. I went to the front and lined up the clients as per my loading list. I asked Denis and another helper, as they had a seating list as well, to go onto to the aircraft and help the clients get in their seats, and help with the overhead luggage (and they had a lot of that). I helped with getting them into the aisle seat. We had a lot of cooperation from special service and the crew, which meant that we loaded the aircraft without any problems; and soon, the rest of the passengers started to board.

Any of them that were near us were having a slight problem finding room in the overhead lockers due to the amount we had—I heard a few of them having a whinge. It wasn't long before the door was shut, and the engines were starting. Soon, we were being pulled back as the engine noise was getting higher. We were now rolling and heading to the runway. The roars of the four jets were pushing you back into your seat, and then the almost magic moment when the aircraft leaves the runway, and you look out of the window to watch things getting smaller. Soon after the seat belt sign went off, around came the drinks trolley. I watched to make sure our clients were getting their drinks, and joined them with a large gin and tonic. I drank it very quickly, and within a few minutes floated off to sleep.

'Terry, Terry,' Dennis was waking me up. 'Sue has taken another woman to the toilet, and the one she is looking after needs to go as well. I told her there wasn't another woman she has asked if you and I can take her.'

Well, I had known this woman for a few years, and she really enjoyed travelling with us. I asked Dennis to get the aisle chair, and we went over to where she was sitting. She had polio and could not stand I got behind her and lifted her up slightly. Dennis got her feet, and we got her on the chair. I then tip the chair slightly, and pulled it backwards heading for the toilets at the rear of the plane. We got to the back and found a free toilet. To everyone who has flown, you must be well aware of just how small these toilets are. You look at it and think, how the hell am I going to do this? I told Dennis I would hold her while he pulled out the side of the aisle chair, he then lifted her feet off the floor; and I carried her backwards into the toilet, and placed her on the toilet seat. This took a lot of effort. As I had been going backward, I had to literally climb to put one of my feet into the sink; and although she was sitting on the toilet, I was totally stuck in there with her. I said to her, 'Mary, I hope you don't want a crap because I am stuck in here with you.'

She was laughing so much that tears were in her eyes. She said, 'I won't be having a crap or indeed anything as I have still got my knickers on.'

I looked down at Dennis as he was in a better position to get them. He looks up at me, but he wasn't laughing. I don't know if it was all the noise we were making, but lucky for us, our helper Sue turned up to finish the job. This was to be just one of the problems toilets were to cause on aircrafts.

During the nine-hour flight, there were many more of our clients using toilets—a lot better than when Dennis and I done it. We were now on our final descent into Orlando International Airport. I had already asked the head steward to contact the ground to make sure our wheelchairs were brought to the gate. The aircraft came to a halt, and the engine noise disappeared. We remained seated, while all the other passengers got up from their seats to open the overhead lockers. It seems to take an age, and I can say over the hundreds of times I have done this it never seems to get any faster. Then the queues on both aisles start to move very slowly toward the door. Soon there is this early sight of an empty jumbo jet with just my group left. I got up from my seat, and walked down to the front door. There is activity going on here as I see our wheelchairs being lined up in the linked corridor. The person who seems to be in charge asks me if I am in charge, and then others appear with two aisle chairs— one for each of the aisles to start the unloading. This is where you have to be careful. All hand luggage comes off of the aircraft to make sure the overhead lockers are empty, and there is a vast amount of it. Dennis and Sue were in the corridor sorting out whose chair was whose, as the special service people were bringing our clients from the aircraft. I had told the special service people that we wanted to go to passport and customs together not separately as it is easier that way. I said our goodbyes to the crew, and thanked them for all of their help.

We started to make our way down to the passport checks and customs area. Anyone reading this that have been to Orlando International Airport will know just how large it is, but this was 1983, and it was not that big then—very much smaller than it is today. We were soon through all the channels, and I was outside looking for the accessible coach. Unfortunately, I soon found it, and it was very old and would not have been allowed in the UK. I had told them how many static wheelchairs we had (people staying in their chairs), but they could only take three instead of six. We started to load, and I asked if I could have volunteers to get out of their wheelchairs until I could get this sorted out. 'It was very hot in the coach,' I said to the driver. 'Could he start it up and put on the air con?'

He said there was none on this vehicle then he started to moan about it saying he hated it, and it was difficult to drive, and all that used it moaned. I asked him if we were his first overseas group, he said yes. I spoke to the group and apologized for the coach, and said I would try to sort this out tomorrow as it was a free day. I was sitting at the back near the lift door with sweat pouring off me talking to some clients when there was a loud bang and crash. I look out of the window and a big lump of the bodywork had dropped off, and was scrapping along the road with other vehicles trying to avoid it. The driver stopped, and got out and put it with the luggage in a side locker. I looked at some of the clients, and started to snigger what a start I thought. We soon arrived at the hotel where I went in with Dennis to get the keys. I helped the driver unload the luggage, and it was in a long line outside the reception. Two other people came out from the hotel with their room lists and trolleys. I went through it with them, and was able to find out who's the luggage was without a label as this often happens. The driver came over and asked me if I had everything, I said it looked like it, and I would see him Wednesday at 9 a.m. for Sea World. I also asked him to sort out the static wheelchairs and he said he would try. He walked back to the coach, and drove past me with a great hole where the bit that fell off should have been.

I went round to see the clients in their rooms to make sure they were okay. All was well, the rooms were nice and accessible and air conditioned, which worked. As this was the US, there were no meals included; and as I was going around, I suggested a place across the road, which I had used a few years ago, and they all agreed. I then thought to myself I hope we will all fit in. Albert was one of the clients on this trip who could wheel himself in his chair, and was on his own in the very large double room. I knocked on the open door, 'Come in, son,' he said. I told him about the restaurant across the road, and asked him if he wanted to come, he said he would love to. I asked him was he sure he was going to able to cope going around theme parks as there was a lot of distance here. He said he would, and there were only certain things he wanted to see. I told him the only reason I was telling him was on the Swiss holiday. I saw one of the cadets pushing him, and there were no cadets here it had all changed now.

I walked across the road to the restaurant hoping they could fit them in. I spoke to the person in charge who reckoned they could, and offered my dinner free of charge (just another little perk). I stayed in the restaurant with a nice cold coke waiting for the group. Dennis was the first with his client, followed by Sue, and hers. Dennis said he would walk back to make sure the others knew where to come. I said I would come with him, and as we went to walk out, there was a sound of a car horn as Albert seemed to have got himself stuck halfway across the road. I pulled him out what seemed to be a small pothole, and got him into the restaurant. I asked him where he wanted to sit, he asked if he could sit with me. I said of course, and took him to my table. I then went back with Dennis to find the rest.

Most of the couples on the tour were married, and had various disabilities—most had strokes and polio. I walked across with a few of the clients then sat down with Albert who had ordered a burger and chips. I did warn him that chips in America are like our crisps. I said you have to ask for fries; he must have done that as chips did come out. Albert was married to Glenis who was also in a wheelchair, and he also had a three-wheeler dangerous car, which Albert would not have said. He loved his little car, we will hear more about his little car as we progress. During the meal, I started to learn a lot about Albert. He had a great sense of humour like me. We were going to become great friends over many years, and this was the start. We all had a great meal, and I talked to all the clients about all the things we would see in the next few weeks.

The next day, I had been for some breakfast, and had been trying to contact the coach company on the telephone for the last hour. I had been promised a call back so had to wait in the room. When they finally got back, they apologized about the three static having to come out of their chairs, but said the sales team should not have told me I could have six static as the coach can only do three. I was fuming, and started to argue with them until the person on the other end basically said take it or leave it. So as it was the only coach with a lift, what do you do now? I really did know what it was like to be disabled. Not many choices!

I thought I would call in to see if Albert was okay. He was sitting in his chair outside his room too bloody hot in their son, he said. I walked in and it was like a sauna. I asked him if it had been like that all night, he said hotter than that. I looked at the air con unit to find it was switched off; I pushed the switch and the fan came roaring on, and it got cooler very quickly. 'You never switched it on,' I told him.

'I never knew it had one,' he said. 'Don't use them in England it's the first one I've seen.'

I looked at him and smiled. He smiled back and said, 'Really, I've never been to countries that use air con.'

I asked him if he had had any breakfast, he said he hadn't so we went across the road.

There were a few of the clients there as well so I told them about my conversation with the coach company, and although some were upset, they could see it was not my fault. Albert was tucking in to a pile of pancakes, which arrived on our table. 'I only ordered fucking one,' he said.

I laughed and said to him, 'Everything is big in America, Albert.'

I later met Dennis, and asked him to inform the clients where and what time to meet tomorrow for our trip to Sea World. I asked Albert what he was going to do as I could see he really wanted some company. I said to him, 'Do you want to come with me? I am going nowhere special, just getting the Disneyworld tickets.'

His face lit up. 'Yes, please,' he said.

During the day, I really got to know Albert; and some of the things he would come out with about all sorts of people, including people in our group, amazed me.

The coach was on time, and we started to load it right away. None of the clients had ever been to Sea World, but I had, so I knew they would be amazed at what they have there and how accessible it is. As we pulled up, I could sense some of the excitement on board. We were soon unloaded, and after confirming our time of pick up, went over to the group and made our way to the entrance. Once in, I gave them all a map of the park each, and told them where to meet at our departure time. Somehow, now I was pushing Albert. Although he did make a good mobile office as he would put my video camera and my brief case on his lap, I thought a good compromise; and as this was 1983, video cameras were not small. One of the good things about Sea World is that it is made up of events so armed with your daily programme, you can go from one to another. The highlight of course is the killer whales and the dolphins. At each event, there are wheelchair spaces so clients with their own helpers could keep together—an idea now of course pretty common—but then, it was indeed very rare. When you enter the event, you see there are areas, which are marked splash zones. They are of course what they say, and they also contain wheelchair spaces in those splash zones. Of course, anyone with any sense goes up higher to avoid the splash zones.

This will always remind me of one of my clients who went on

holiday with us for many years who I have sadly missed since her death, as she became a great friend of my wife and me. She had a sight problem, and could only see anything directly in front of her. When she first came with us, she came on her own, and used to hold onto the handle of a wheelchair when we went out on excursions. This time, on the Orlando holiday once again, we were in Sea World to see the killer whale show. The lady in question, Norma, was with my wife and myself. We walked up to the top way out of the splash zone where we all sat down. I saw there was popcorn for sale, and asked my wife Marian if she wanted any. She said she would come with me and left Norma sitting. Whilst we were getting the popcorn, the show begun, and this extremely large whale came out splashing its way around the huge pool. The water was coming over the sides, and splashing most of the people sitting in the splash zones. Then something very strange happened. It hit the water so hard, a lump of water sped up in the air, and I could see this was going way past the splash zone; and it did, and the whole lot landed on Norma who of course could not have seen it coming. Well, the language turned the air blue even the whale must have heard her as he went under water for a few minutes. She was totally soaked. Marian was trying to get something to dry her off, but she thought Marian and I had set her up that's why we left her on her own. Although she spoke to Marian, she didn't speak to me for a day.

We were soon making our way back to the entrance/exit to load the coach for our return for what was a very successful day—except for Norma—but she later saw the funny side of things. The next day was a rest day, or for many people, a shopping day. Things were pretty cheap in the states at that time, and many people would get the bargains with trainers; and of course, those expensive jeans in the UK, but not here at that time. I remember saying to some of the clients, remember we are flying back, and to watch the weight of the cases as the luggage was getting more and more.

That evening after dinner, a group of us were sitting outside having a few drinks. I think people were winding down knowing things were okay, and were more relaxed and really enjoying this type of holiday. People were beginning to open up and talk more about their disability, and to someone like me, I was starting to see through the disability to the person they were.

Around the table were Albert, who we already know now or so we thought; Mike, who has cerebral palsy and has to walk with his arms out to keep his balance, and when he talks, it is very difficult to understand him. Dennis, who is one of my helpers; and Joe, who was being looked after by him. It was a very pleasant evening, and the drinks were going down quickly without much effort. As time passed, the subjects were getting more open until it comes to women. Joe really did like a drink, and got through quite a bit during the day. He also used to smoke about sixty cigarettes a day. He lost his legs in an accident—he was drunk at the time. He told me it was a good thing that he was as he didn't feel much pain. I told him if he had been sober, the accident wouldn't have happened. 'I never thought about it that way,' he said laughing.

Joe went on many holidays with us, and money never seemed to be a problem as he used to shop for good quality and expensive clothing. Some very funny things have happened over the years. Joe looked at Albert and said, 'You're married. Do you need any help when you do it?'

'You're a nosey bugger,' he said.

'Don't you worry, son. I manage when needed.'

Joe looked at Albert and said, 'Sorry Albert, I didn't want to upset you.'

'Don't worry about me, son,' he said. 'I didn't go short when I was single, and I certainly don't now.'

Albert took a swig of his brandy, and looks around and said, 'Any of you gone to a lady of the night?'

'What a prostitute,' said Denis.

'I was trying to be polite,' said Albert. I have, and I tell you it is all business disability don't count.'

'What do you mean?' I said.

'Well, a friend of mine many years ago who also had polio told me that he went to one, and asked if I wanted to use her. At the time, I didn't think I could handle it. Anyway, as time went on, I decided to go so ask my friend for the address. I got there, and what he didn't tell me was it was right at the top of the stairs. Well, going back to those years, I only used my two sticks and was much faster. Anyway, I got to the top and rang the bell. The madam opened it, asked me to come in, and showed me into this women's room. Well, unlike many of you here, it takes me ten minutes to get my boots off, and she charged me waiting time.' Well everyone started laughing.

Albert looked at us all and said, 'Really, she did? She said it isn't her fault it took so long to get your boots off. I have other clients, and time is money. Nothing to do with your disability, it's business.'

Mike was laughing so much he had tears in his eyes. He asked whose round it was. We told him it was his so he went to get up, and fell backward back into his chair. 'Are you alright?' I asked.

Mike looked at me and said, 'I look the same drunk as I do sober. Something you can't do,' he said. 'And I get away with it.'

Not only could he get away with it many times when he did go up to the bar he was asked for his ID, and he is older than me. Mike has also been on holiday with us more than any other customer. He started in 1980, and has been every year up to 2012. I have learned a lot from Mike, as he must be the most frustrated man in the world. He is a very clever man. In fact, he has many degrees from history to art, but when he tries to talk to people, he is mostly ignored; and as I have seen many times, treated as a fool. He tends to cough and dribble a lot when he is eating, so many times I would be on his table or people that knew him. I remember an occasion at one hotel, which upset me. When I started operating holidays, I wanted to upgrade them and use four-star hotels wherever possible. On this occasion, we had checked in, and we had gone into the very nice restaurant for dinner. It was quite full, and during the meal, I saw people looking at Mike whilst he was eating. Then I saw some of the guests talking to the head waiter. The next morning after breakfast, we started to load the coach when one of the managers came over to me, and asked if he could have a word. He said that he could arrange for Mike to have the à la carte menu and free drinks in his room for the rest of the stay to save him having to come to the restaurant as he was sure it would make it easier for him. I knew exactly what he meant, but he hadn't thought it out. I said, 'That is a very kind offer, and I am sure Mike would appreciate it. Nevertheless, poor Mike spends most of his time at home on his own. When he comes on holiday, he comes for the company. But I tell you what, up the end of the restaurant there is a table for two. If Mike sits facing me, his back will be to the restaurant, and no one will see him. So tonight, we will both have the à la carte menu, and of course a bottle of champagne. I think that will solve your problem with some of your other guests, will it not?'

He looked at me and smiled, 'I think it will.'

That incident showed me how it would take a few years until attitudes changed, and until then, more education and subtlety would be needed. I can quite understand the attitude of this hotel and its clientele. They had never seen this before, I showed them, there were ways to get round it. What surprised me more were the attitudes by some disabled people to other disabled people. I know that some clients stopped coming with us because they couldn't cope with some of our other client's disability. This will always happen when you operate escorted tours where you make up a group, as by its nature, you will attract all types of people. Over the past thirty years, there has been a considerable improvement, but even now I still see some resistance.

The next day was our first day at Disneyworld. We pulled away on time, and were heading to the Magic Kingdom. On arrival, we unloaded the coach, and I made a time for pick up with the driver. We made our way to the boat, which would take us to the kingdom—this was designed like the Mississippi river boats. The whole of the park was designed with great thought, and even the lake we were on was man-made.

When we got off the boat, the entrance was in front. I had already got some maps, which showed all of the accessible rides ECT. I had a word with the group and told them that it is better not to go around in a large group, and the time to meet where the coach would be. I took Albert, and usually, Dennis would have followed me with his client; but as you can imagine, Joe would rather have a drink than go to a Magic Kingdom with no alcohol. In the early days at Disneyworld, if you were a wheelchair user, you went to the front of the queue, and the person with you would have to get you in and out of the ride—not the Disney staff. I asked Albert what he wanted to go on, but he wasn't very adventurous, I asked if he wanted me to push him, we had to go on as many as possible so I could tell other clients what the ride was like. And the first ride was coming up. By the end of the day, Albert had been on nearly all the rides; and although he wouldn't admit it, he did enjoy it and his favourite ride was the Pirates of the Caribbean.

The next day, it was Epcot (Experimental Prototype Community of Tomorrow). I would say this was my favourite park. For this park, we had left later as every evening there are fireworks and laser show, so we won't be back at the coach until at least 10.45 that evening. Once again, I had spoken to the group, and armed them with their maps. I also told them they had a unique choice of eating places that evening, as there are twelve countries built around the lake, and each one has staff born in that country plus food from there as well. I took Albert again and surprise Joe was here with Denis. Well what can you get in the restaurants? Yes, drinks! As Dennis and Joe went off to the countries, Albert and I went around the universes—the first one being the universe of energy. This is a visual experience including being roared at by dinosaurs, but very well done. We did all the universes,

41

and even Space Mountain as we made our way over to the countries around the lake. As we had booked dinner at China for 7 p.m., we started with Canada, which was the other direction so being a circle around the lake would bring us to China at the right time. As we were going from country to country, we would often see members of our group enjoying the atmosphere of the events. For those of you reading this and that have seen the fireworks and lasers at Epcot, you will know what I mean when I say you really have to see this to believe it as words really can't describe what you see and experience.

The time had come for us to check out of the hotel in Orlando for our transfer to Miami. I had been assured that the coach had been repaired, and bits put back where they had fell off. The entire luggage had been bought to the front of the hotel, and the clients were still finishing their breakfast when the coach turned up. I told the clients not to rush, and we would start loading once we had taken care of the luggage. We were soon on our way down to Miami. The coach was very hot as it had no air con. I had already talked to the driver about how long it would take, and how many stops we would need. My shirt was wet with sweat as were some of our clients. Every-time I went to see if they were okay, the first question was when are we were going to stop.

We pulled into what looked like a service area, stopped, and started to unload. I told the clients that once we unloaded, I would come over so we would know what time to load again. We were halfway through unloading when I noticed that the lift platform was full of ants—and rather large ants at that. One of the clients that had just got off the lift started screaming as they were on her feet, and starting to go up her leg. Her husband and Sue were trying to get them off, and clear her from the coach. It turns out the driver had pulled up where the lift was coming down on the dirt instead of the concrete. I told him to move the coach up. He pulled up the lift, and went into the coach. He pushed the start button, and nothing happened. So now I have clients stuck on a coach that now won't move, and the only way to get them off would be through the ants' nest. I told the driver to fill up his water container that I had seen in the locker so we could get the ants off the lift platform. It took a few containers full, but it seemed to be working. We started to unload, and soon had the clients off the coach. I said to the driver to contact his office, and sort out what had to be done to get us to Miami.

I walked away and joined the clients. As soon as I walked in, the air con hit me and I started to cool down. As you can imagine, the clients were not much pleased. I told them neither was I. It seemed strange to some of our clients that they had seen so much accessibility in and around Disney (including their transport) and yet, all I was providing them with was rubbish. I agreed it seemed that way, and showed them telephone numbers of the tourist boards in Orlando and Miami. I said I would gladly contact them so they could speak to them directly to see about accessible private coach hire, and they would be told that this was the only company providing this. Things were different in most other countries, and some had yet to recognize the growing accessible market, how long it had taken me to get started, and some of the attitudes I had to put up with—and still did. The driver appeared and came over to me (I could tell by his face it was not going to be good news). The coach would have to get back to their depot for repair so all that could be offered was a standard coach with no lift. There were a few of my clients who were not happy, and said how ridiculous it was not having spares. I told them that would come with time, but now was now and we had to cope with it now.

I went and told the others of the group what was happening and we waited for the replacement coach. It seems very strange now, but back in 1983, this is how it was—there were very few accessible coaches. Back in the UK, I was still the only commercial operator, and we only had five. There were others, but they belonged to charities, and the operating laws meant they could not be used for hire and reward. We would spend many hours sending faxes and letters as well as many expensive telephone calls to overseas agents trying to find accessible coaches. There wasn't cheap email then, this was something that would cause a revolution in finding and explaining access in the future.

The coach finally turned up, and we had to start carrying people up the stairs into the coach. We were finally off on our way to Miami.

I used the microphone on the coach to explain to the clients the best I could about the coach, and that although there were no excursions planned for the Miami section, I could offer one free of charge; but it would not be on the one and only accessible coach. The air con was working very well, and the clients' mood seemed to be getting better.

Our hotel was on the beach, and was a nice place to relax as well as the shopping area just a few minutes away. There were also many restaurants and fast food outlets. We were on a bed and breakfast basis in our hotel so the choice was good. Many of the clients ate in the hotel that evening, and I joined them with Albert. It is very handy having Albert because as he is also a client, he could speak to other clients as a client who had also paid and explain how hard I was trying to get these to work. Many of the clients were talking about a visit to Cape Kennedy as it was something they had always seen on television, and would love to see it in reality.

The following day, I made some calls and spoke to the Cape. There was no problem for wheelchair users—even the bus was accessible—and the person I was talking to seemed very excited about their coach. I thought when I hung up, it would seem a bit strange if you could send a man to the moon, but not have a vehicle to take wheelchairs. I informed the clients that were interested, and made the arrangements. In the end, they all went which was good.

The day of the excursion arrived, and I saw this very large new coach arrive outside. I went over to the coach to make sure the coach was for us, which it was. It was very cold inside the coach, and that was a good start. We were soon loaded, and on our way, the driver was excellent. He knew the history of the area, and what had happened there. He also knew a lot about the cape as he had done many trips there before. I sat back in my seat and thought, *thank goodness.*

On arrival, the driver showed me where the office was, and where he would be when we were ready to go back to the hotel. The system was good at the Cape. I got a group ticket, and they asked what time I would like the bus, as we were the only ones on it. I arranged for it to pick us up one hour later for a snack, and the ever- important toilets, which were accessible. The coach was not a touring coach but practical, and had the room for wheelchairs. We had a guided tour, and then went back to the starting point where there were all sorts of shops and a 3D film showing a take- off and floating in space. It really was something unique then, which all the clients enjoyed. Our trip back to the hotel was a happy one; there was a good atmosphere even though we had to lift the clients on and off the coach again.

The rest of the holiday was more of a relaxed time, but the departure day soon came around, and we loaded the coach for the last time. I had already spoken to Denis and Sue so we all knew what we would be doing. We arrived at the airport right outside the check in counters. I went in with the tickets, and the driver was getting the luggage off with help of the airport porters. I learned over the few years I had been running holidays that overseas, airports are different from UK ones, and tipping is very important so you must bear that in mind.

Check in was very quick and easy. We were soon on our way through security and passport control. I sat having a drink with Albert, Joe, and Denis. I asked both Albert and Joe if they had a good time; they said it was better than they could ever have imagined 'Are you serious?' I said. And they were. They didn't want it to end, but end it did twelve hours later.

The first day back in the office, I spent an hour talking to the coach operator in Orlando wanting a great deal of the money back. We argued for a while then agreed a price. I said that he should take advantage of what he had, and where he was. He was in the theme park capital of the world, with at the time, the only accessible coach; but if he was to continue, he had to buy a newer one that worked with air con. He didn't, and there are now much more and better accessible coaches in Florida. When planning Europe tours, I often wanted to fly, but there just wasn't any accessible transport anywhere at the time; and to this day, there still aren't many accessible tour coaches. So all European tours for the time being had to be with our coaches.

I had put together a small team in the office. My holiday officer was Pat, a lady who used to work on school transport for the council dealing with children with disability. I also had another person on transport as we still did many school contracts—home to school transport.

We were only a few weeks away from sending out the 1984 brochure, which would include many coach holidays, and some flights where we had found some sort of transport. This would include Orlando once again so I was already worried about the transport situation. We now started to get requests from charities who would want us to put together holidays using our transport. They then used to arrange events to raise the money needed. They found this to be much cheaper than having their own transport, and on some occasions, we would lower the prices if they used a time slot when our vehicles were not being used then everyone gained.

Bill was now our paid consultant, and I used to enjoy his visits. Mind you, we didn't always see eye to eye; but even though Bill was working and involved with charities most of his life, he still had a commercial streak in him which did surprise me sometimes. I remember going on trips with him where he used to give talks to various bodies. One was an ABTA talk I think in Bournemouth. He said to one of the organizers that when he was introduced, he would like to walk on in his own way to show the audience how he walked, and somehow kept his balance. The only problem was that he was due to walk on from the side of the stage right on the edge, and I thought that was a bit dangerous. The reason being that if you hadn't seen Bill walk it was hard to imagine. Because of Bills CP, he had to swing himself side by side to move forward, and he had to go at a certain speed so he didn't lose his balance. The problem was when he stopped, he had to hold something otherwise he could—and often did—fall over. I said to Bill, 'Do you think that is a good idea because what happens when you stop on the stage to give your talk.'

'That's alright,' he said.

Because the microphone is there any way he had made up his mind that the audience should see his problems. I was now sitting in the audience when the person came over to the microphone to tell us about Bill's history in taking disabled people in wheelchairs on holiday, the problems that faced him, and how he had got over them. Bill then made his entrance. I looked up at him; he was a bit jerkier than normal. He grabbed hold of the microphone stand, and it slipped away from him. I got up to get over to the stage. At the same time, there was this great sigh of concern. As I got there, Bill had got back on his balance, and started to make a joke out of it. Everyone started to clap, and of course, Bill had made his point. I really enjoyed being in his company, and going on speaking trips with him. It was always an adventure, and it really helped when you were talking to hoteliers and transport operators. Things were beginning to happen. There was more understanding, and it was starting to create a new market of travellers. You could feel it as well as seeing it, and so could Bill. He said to me one day that all his life he had been waiting for this new horizon in travel, and he knew now he would see it in his lifetime.

We both realized that the future would be total access where someone who used a wheelchair would not feel out of place, but he also knew you had to have a sense of humour to cope with some of the events that would happen. Bill had this all his life, which had helped him cope—others could find it more difficult. He said to me, 'You sometimes have a wicked sense of humour, but you seem to get away with it. Don't stop improving this leisure business, please keep on until it is all one.'

Well, I have and it nearly is. Of course, it still has some way to go but since 1980, it has changed so much.

CHAPTER 4

O ver the next few years, we became known for our accessible transport and holiday provision, and smaller accessible vehicles started to be added to our operator's fleet. Some new operators started up just supplying wheelchair accessible vehicles. We had an advantage as we were the first, and of course, had gained a great deal more experience as we supplied holidays as well. We were also able to find more accessible transport in other countries, which included Orlando, and at last, Europe. Also, there were more agents in Europe and the States who specialised in accessible holidays. I got to know Dominic an agent in France who was himself disabled, and organized trips into France. He would supply the hotels and ground arrangements, and I would supply the transport, and of course the customers. He then started to sell the UK to his clients, and we would send one of our coaches over to France to pick up then run the tour in the UK and return them to France. This was a good arrangement, and my first experience with disabled people from other countries; and what they looked for in access, which I have found very interesting. Dominic would come over to the UK, and sometimes stay with me, and we would plan out tours both for French and Brits. I learned that lunch for French clients was of great importance, and should always run an itinerary around this important event. Between us, we put together some very good itineraries, which sold well for a few years. Over the years to come, many other people from around the world started up agencies for people with disabilities.

When planning and making itineraries, there is a golden rule as the three most import factors are *toilets*, *toilets*, and *toilets*. Every hotel used must have these not only in the room, but where possible in the hotel itself. Many new operators that come along would look at this, but many seemed to forget when they went on an excursion. This was very important as it could ruin a good excursion. When we researched the holidays, we would look where the excursion would be, and then look around where the nearest accessible toilet was— of course, in the early days this was very difficult as finding toilets was a near impossible task. Where we could find no accessible toilets, we would look for the biggest ones that we could use. When going on the excursion, we would point this out to the clients so they were aware. Sometimes, they would come back from the excursion telling me they had found other ones, and I would always say the more the merrier. At least, I would trust this information as it would be correct unlike information you would sometimes get from tourist information offices.

There was a great shortage of access information at tourist offices worldwide—that was because they had never been asked for it before. Charities were the main tour operators for disabled people. They had transport and accommodation, and every year they would take their people away. This meant on many occasions that CP went with CP, and so on. As I have said, it surprised me on some of the attitudes of some disabled people against other disabled. And as our tours expanded, it would be inevitable that we would take all sorts of disability. This did happen, and it also coincided with us taking clients from America on UK and European holidays.

This was a very interesting project. I found the American clients during this time period so much happier and grateful for any help that we gave them. Many clients from the UK expected us to help in certain ways even though we didn't have to, whereas the American clients really appreciated the service. This also showed itself at the end of a holiday when much of the time, many of our staff did not receive any form of gratuity after all the non-paid work that they had done, whereas of course the Americans were very grateful. I don't believe it was because our clients were mean in any way, it was the way it was—it was just expected.

The other precious thing on all excursions was time as this was always in short supply on excursions. Depending on the excursion, leaving at the crack of dawn was not an option as it could take some of our clients a long time to get ready. Also, there was breakfast and after the loading of the coach, which all took time. When planning the holiday, I would go from the hotel to the excursion venue in my car if it were in the UK or Europe, and test the travelling time also to see if it was longer than two hours, and if there were toilets we could use. Even though we had toilets on our coaches, we would still have to stop, and would take a long time if more than one wanted to go. As you can imagine, excursions come in many forms. They can be tours where you pick up a guide or places you visit such as factories, stately homes, etc. Nevertheless, there has to be toilets either public or in the building you are visiting.

From all the information gained in the planning, there then is the putting together of the brochure, we would allow three to four months for this. We had to plan what pictures would be used, and to make sure none of them had any copyright. Our mailing list had grown, and we had about 5,000 more on it in 1990. From when we started the holidays in 1980, during that ten-year period, we had seen changes for the better happening. There were more hotels and more toilets at last, and we started looking at much further locations including Singapore, Malaysia, New Zealand, and Australia.

Australia was interesting as I went there with Albert in 1986 to the ABTA convention. I thought it would be great to see, and of course for Albert, a dream. I also wanted to see how they would cope, and of course they didn't. I worked out an itinerary for us which would take in Perth, Sydney, and where the convention was the Gold Coast. Although ABTA did most of the reservations, I spoke to the airline as there are a row of seats that are ideal for Albert, as during the flight, he tends to slip down the seat due to the fact he can't bend his legs; and because there are no passengers behind, it means I can go behind him and lift him back up—over a long flight, it is important as I have seen him with his chin resting on the chair table. The day dawned when one of my vehicles picked up Albert and myself, and took us to Heathrow—only having Albert to look after would be like a holiday to me or so I thought. I took Albert to the BA check in where I told them about my conversation with their reservations, and why I needed those seat numbers only to be told those seats had already been taken. I asked them if the passengers allocated the seats had a disability, they said no, but they wanted those seats. I said reservations had told me they were available so someone is lying. No effort was made to change the situation, in fact, it seemed we were being ignored, which of course we were. We boarded the aircraft, and once again, I tried to change our seats to no avail.

The flight was London–Kuwait–Perth, and we were soon travelling down the runway and taking off over London. There was nothing unusual about the flight, just the predictable drinks trolley, then dinner; and by this time, Albert's chin is not far from his dinner. Tried to lift him, but could only lift slightly on one side. I was also trapped because of the seat tray tables, and even if I did get into the aisle, I would not have been able to get behind him as there were people sitting there. One of the stewards was passing so I called him over to show him Albert's predicament. He arranged for the people behind to move out of their seats, while I went behind to lift him up. The steward said he would see what he could do when we landed, as there would be a crew change.

When we boarded again, which was usually always first, we were shown into the seat we wanted. I asked the new steward how he did this, and he said he just asked the passengers who were there if they would mind moving and they agreed. It seems the other steward never asked, and all of Albert's uncomfortable flight could have been avoided. Over the years, I was to see this behaviour many times with many airlines because it was like they never listened or wanted to.

The next leg of the flight went smoothly, and during those hours, I adjusted Albert about six times as well as his toilet trips. In fact, when we landed, I was worn out. When flying with a group, this section seemed to take ages (getting ten wheelchair users off the aircraft through customs and immigration, getting the luggage, and then finding our transport). Well, at least once again I only had Albert.

As the last passenger before us left the aircraft, I saw Albert's wheelchair in the pier. I went over to check it, and someone asked if I needed any help getting him off. I thanked them, but said I would be fine. I went back, and helped Albert to his chair. Once in, I then loaded him up with our hand luggage. As you can imagine, this was a fair amount, so much so you couldn't see Albert. He was like my moving luggage trolley. We went through the immigration and customs, and collected the luggage, which did cause a problem, as no one was around to help. So I had the luggage trolley in one hand, and Albert in the other making my way out of the terminal to find the coach. I saw someone standing with a board saying ABTA and went over. He asked for my name and ticked it from his clip board. There were a few gathering around him, and one of them asked if he could help with pushing the chair. We made our way over to the coach where people were already on board, and of course, all the front seats were taken. I knew although Albert could stand, he could not climb stairs. I got him to stand by the entrance then lifted him up one by one—still no one offered to move—and it then took a few minutes while he moved down the aisle to the seat.

People started to introduce themselves who were sitting around us, some seeming concerned that no one offered to move from the front seats. The journey to our hotel was good, and we learned a lot about Perth and the hotel we were going to stay at for the next couple of days. We had arrived during the Americas cup, and the Australian entry was funded by Alan Bond whose company owned the hotel where we would be. After check in, we were all very tired, and went to our rooms.

Breakfast was interesting, and we started to meet many ABTA members, also as you can imagine, people were interested in who Albert was, and what he was doing at the convention. I told them that he worked for me as an access consultant, and wanted to see—like me—what people knew about access; and more importantly, what they were going to do about it. Albert seemed to become a little celebrity. I would look around, and someone would be pushing Albert away in his chair, and having a drink with them. I asked the rep about accessible buses and coaches, and he told me there wasn't any that he knew about although he knew of one that belonged to a charity. I asked where disabled people went on holiday, and he didn't seem to know.

We left Perth, and went to Sydney before ending up at the convention hotel at the Gold Coast minus our luggage, which was on a train coming from Sydney as it was put on the wrong coach. The hotel was very good about it, and let us use the shops in the resort to buy things we would need until our luggage arrived the next day. The hotel was also a casino which Albert had not seen before. He was also unaware that when you gambled on the television, it was real; the money you won would be credited to your room, but if you lost you would have to pay. Luckily, Albert had won a few dollars.

Now we were at the Convention hotel. The entire ABTA delegates were here, and it was very interesting meeting these people. Also, we had many conversations about accessible holidays, and I was also able to talk to many hoteliers who could see there was money in providing these services. There were a few well known people such as the late Henry Cooper and Judith Chalmers. On the official opening, there was one area, which I thought deserved a visit that was where the airlines were to be found. I made my way to British Airways with Albert to make an official complaint; of course, they were sorry, and they would make sure they interviewed all concerned on the first leg of the flight. They asked if we were flying back to the UK with them, I told them we were with Qantas, and they had guaranteed our seats.

It was my first ABTA convention, and I was impressed with the arrangements that were made at the convention itself. A day at an animal park just for the delegates went down very well. The good thing was it was accessible, and I was able to show Albert all that was there without any problems. Well, I say everything there was, however, something that could have caused a problem. Albert likes kangaroos, and wanted his picture taken with one. As we were walking round the park, we saw one by itself in an enclosure. Albert pointed this out, and said push me in so I am next to it, and then take a photo. We went up to the gate, and pushed it open—I thought it was a bit stiff. Anyway, we got in and made our way to the kangaroo that was drinking. It didn't seem to be bothered, and was ignoring us. I parked Albert by him, and took a photo. He turned and looked down at Albert. There was then a shout from someone to get out of there— it was a ranger who kept beckoning us out. As we got to the gate he said, 'Can't you read? You must not go in there that is not the docile kangaroo you see on television, it's a red they can kill you.' It was a good job it wasn't hungry but we were, and made our way back for lunch.

During our next few days, we met many tour operators and travel agents who were all interested in disabled people going on holidays. I said that Australia would be a good location as it was a new country, and didn't need much to make things accessible. It was also showing people the size of the market worldwide, which certainly is eye-opening. Albert and I also got to know some of the hotel staff, which is the real way to meet people in the country you are in.

One afternoon, some were off work and invited us to go out with them, which we gladly accepted. One of them had an estate car, which was ideal. I got Albert in the front seat with the driver who happened to be a really nice young lady, while I sat in the back with the other two men. They asked where we would like to go, I said just show us Surfers Paradise—places where the tourist don't usually go. She certainly did, and I really loved what I saw; and I was getting very attracted to Australia, and Albert to the driver. We ended up in a bar in a shopping complex, and talked all night. It was really great. We decided we had had enough, and time to get back to the hotel. I took Albert to the lift where I found, to my horror, they had been turned off, and the only way down was the escalator. Our new friends had forgotten—as they of course always used the stairs— they had forgotten about the wheelchair. I had taken a chair down on an escalator before so I tipped Albert backwards, and down we went. The time had come to fly back to the UK. When we checked in,

Qantas had made sure we had the seats we needed, and it was a good flight back.

Going to the ABTA convention made more people take notice of the travel needs of disabled people, and of course, the more that knew the more things would change. It was time to get back, and continue getting the message out.

The holidays had been selling well, and we had a Singapore and Malaysia trip organized for later that year. It was our furthest trip yet, and we had arranged this through the tourist board. I knew they did not have an accessible coach, and we would have to lift people on, but had made this clear in the information on the holiday. I knew many of the people who were on the trip (including Albert) so I knew their disabilities. We had a group of nineteen pax, and all met up at Heathrow where we all got to know each other at the check in. Before the EU became involved, each airline had their own what was called special services, which were responsible for getting you to and on the aircraft—and all in all did a fair job. Although as more and more disabled people started to travel and demand a higher standard of service, many more mistakes were made leading to more and more complaints, but that was yet to come. We all arrived at the departure gate, and were taken down the tunnel to the aircraft door. There, the special service staff had the on board chair ready. 'Who can walk to their seats?' asked the man in charge. I said I would help get those seated and pointed to Albert, and asked him to take Albert to his seat first. Within a few minutes, all the walkers were in their seats, and the non-walkers were being brought to their seats. The crew were then getting ready for boarding, and sure enough, it wasn't long before the plane was filling up. Soon, the plane was full, and all of the overhead lockers were starting to close. The chief steward started to talk to welcome us aboard for our first leg of the flight to Dubai. I checked with my staff to ensure all our clients were okay, and got the thumbs up. So time to sit back in my seat, and get ready for take-off.

One of the things I enjoyed about flying was the take-off. I think it must be the power of the jets and how it lifts this great machine into the air. I must have passed this excitement on to my eldest son as he become, and still is, an air steward. This was going to be a good trip as most clients had their own helper, so apart from Albert and one other, that's all the personal care we had to give. Of course, there was still the running of the holiday.

Dubai came and went without any problems. We were now getting ready for landing at Singapore, and all our clients were ready. I called over the steward to make sure our wheelchairs were bought up to the gate after the rest of the passengers had left the aircraft. I got up from my seat and walked to the door chatting to the stewards. I saw a group of eight to ten people bringing our wheelchairs up the corridor. I used to smoke at that time and really wanted to light one up, but that was at least one hour away—lots to do yet. I stood talking to the aircrew, whilst I was waiting for everyone to get off the aircraft. To empty a jumbo jet seems to take forever, especially when you want a cigarette that must be the same today. At last, the plane was empty with just us left. I told the wheelchair staff who should come off first, but of course they got it wrong. We were then making our way to the immigration and customs area. The people at immigration were amazed that people in wheelchairs had come all this way to Singapore, and I am sure some had not seen a wheelchair before. We continued through to the luggage collection then customs, and the fun part, locating the coach. As I walked out through customs with Albert, I saw someone standing with a notice, which said Chalfont Line. I went over to the lady, and introduced myself. She asked if we were all together, and we made our way to the coach park. I knew the coach had no lift so Tom who was one of my drivers and me would lift the clients on.

Things went very smoothly, and while the clients were being loaded, the driver was loading the entire luggage. I hadn't noticed how sticky it was outside until I got inside the coach, and felt the air conditioning. Singapore was very humid and hot, and I began to wonder how we would cope on some of the excursions planned. The person from the tourist board also acted as a guide from the airport to the hotel, which for the ones that kept awake was interesting. The hotel was fine, very large, and on the outskirts. I had arranged only bed and breakfast so the clients could choose when and what they wanted to eat. Everyone was tired even though it was midday here. I took Albert to our room where he wanted to lay on the bed for a few hours. I had a shower, and went down to see if there were any of our clients around, there wasn't; so I sat in a nice comfortable chair, and went to sleep.

About two hours went by when I felt someone pressing my neck. It was one on my clients Jane who I heard say, 'I think he's awake now.' I looked round, and she was behind me in her chair with her friend who had come with her to help. We started to talk, and ordered a drink and a sandwich. We started talking about the excursions and the timings. I told them that if we all met at the pool in a couple of hours, I would go through the timings, and I would telephone the others in the group as to where we would meet up.

I walked back to the room, and Albert had got up and was having a wash. He said he had been reading about the facilities in the hotel, and was interested in having a massage. I told him that I was going to arrange to meet the clients around the pool to go through the itinerary with them. He said I could tell him that anytime. I said, 'I know why you want to go for a massage. It's because you think it's something else you will get.' He looked and laughed. I said, 'Get ready, and I will take you down.'

We arrived at the reception, and I booked him in. He had his swimming trunks on, and a hotel dressing gown. I asked the girl if they needed any help, and they looked him over and put her hands in the air and said, 'No.'

The group was either in the pool or sitting around relaxing. I had told them the times we would be departing, and some of the things we would be doing. I looked at the clock, and thought I would go down to collect Albert. I walked in to see Albert sitting in his chair with the foot rests of his wheelchair scattered around the floor with towels and creams. He looked embarrassed, as did the three—yes, three—girls around him trying to work out how the footrests fitted on the chair. I picked them up, and fitted them back on the chair. I said thanks to the girl (I had yet to find out why), and pushed him out to the pool where the rest of the group were sitting around the table. I ordered us both a drink and went to my seat. Janet, Jane's friend, looked at Albert and asked how he got on. He looked at her and laughed, 'Getting on was okay, it was the getting off that was the problem.'

Janet looked at him and then me. 'Don't ask me, Janet,' I said.

It was just then that one of the girls from the massage centre appeared, and came over to me. She said, 'Him not pay.'

I said, 'No, don't worry. It goes on his room bill.'

She looked around and said, 'No, him have special and not pay.'

I looked around, and saw the group sniggering. I put Albert back in his chair, and took him back to the massage parlour under protest of course.

We were all having breakfast the next morning when the lady from the tourist board arrived. I left the group, and went to join her on the settee in the lounge. She told me it was the zoo today, and had brought with her a map for everyone. I asked about steps, and she said there were none at the zoo. She also said there was a public bus that went straight to the zoo so she had arranged no cost for transport that day. What she didn't say was the coach went around all the hotels first, which put a good hour and a half on the trip; and because the door was open, a lot of the time the heat was overtaking the air con. When we got to the zoo, I telephoned her, and said I wanted a vehicle just for us to go back to the hotel. Once out in the open, it was very hot and humid. We decided to go around as a group just in case we come across other things we should have been told about. It wasn't long before we found out there were lots of hills, and pushing chairs uphill in that heat takes it out of you. Nevertheless, we did the zoo, and had our own transport back to the hotel.

The next day after breakfast, I was sitting in the lounge waiting for the tourist board lady to arrive, as she was coming with us today to see what it was like to take people in wheelchairs on excursions. Today, we were going on a coach to the docks where we would board a boat to go to an island, have a tour, and then come back by cable car—just a normal simple excursion! She arrived, and made a big mistake as she asked how the trip to the zoo went, so I told her! Once again, I asked about steps and hills now. She said she could see no problems today. The coach arrived, and after boarding, made our way to the docks. There was no problem boarding, and we're soon on our way to the island. I couldn't believe how many ships there were, moored around the harbour. As the island got closer, I could see the cable car above, and thought that will be interesting. The boat started to pull into the small harbour. I could see some coaches there, and I said to the guide did she know which one was ours. 'Yes,' she said. 'The big red one over there, and they come from London.'

It was an old route master with a platform, no air con, and of course difficult to get on. Nevertheless, we did get on and went round the island, which was very interesting. When we stopped for a drink, the guide arranged for it to be bought out to us on the bus. She thought, of course she was trying to help, but forgot about the toilet so we had to get off anyway. I got off to take Albert as he can manage on his own. I sat down and had a coffee with the guide, and we started talking about what you have to look at when arranging holidays and tours for people with disabilities. I told her that we pay more than most for our clients as we need more facilities, but I hoped as time went on, more and more facilities would become available and bring the cost down. If we want to take clients away from the UK, we have to trust people in those countries for us to research would cost money making it more expensive. Of course, with my experience in what the UK had to offer, I was able to give overseas agents information I had gained

We were now making our way to the cable car, which I could see on the top of the hill. I looked over at the guide. 'Now, are you sure there are no steps?' I said.

'No, defiantly not,' she said.

I had my doubts. The coach pulled up outside, and I went through to see who was correct. It was the guide; I was glad to say. The cars weren't very big; they would only carry two at a time. Tom and I started to help our client onto the cars. I put Albert on last, as I would be in with him. The guide took the car behind me. It wasn't a long crossing, and many years later, this same cable car would be hit by a large ship from below.

As we got nearer, I could see all our clients waiting. As I was helping Albert, Tom came over to tell me the bad news. Although there were no steps up to the cable car, there was quite a few to get down to the waiting coach. By this time, the guide had arrived and had got out of the car. I told her we had a problem. She was genuinely shocked, and I could see by her face she really didn't know what to do. I looked at the steps, and spoke to Tom and Janet; and because there wasn't that many that needed lifting, we decided we would do it only if the clients agreed. If not, we would have to go back, and on the London bus back to the ferry. They all agreed, and we went to work. People who could walk even a short distance first, last the ones that couldn't. It didn't take that long, and without incident, we were soon on the coach on our way back to the hotel. The guide was very quiet on the way back, and I told her I would speak to her on her own later.

We soon unloaded, and all of the clients went to their rooms to get ready for dinner later. I went into the cafe part of the hotel with the guide for a coffee and a chat. She apologized about the steps, and said she wasn't told, and couldn't understand why the tourist office didn't think about it. I said it was simple. They had never been asked to handle wheelchairs before, and mistakes will be made; but not on the cable car as this will now be documented for others to see, but there will be many others in the future. I told her that I would send her a report on the holiday so it could be used in the future, and I would only be too happy to answer questions from their office so they could handle future tours, and even advertise worldwide, they could do this. I told them this would increase their revenue, and help not just disabled people. In the future as people got older there would be more accessible travel; not only on road transport, but trains and hopefully, the air.

The following day was a free day, and clients who had their own helper went off to explore. I had some bookwork to do to get ready for tomorrow's flight to Penang, and also we had an evening dinner cruise. Albert had decided to have another massage, I told him to make sure he took some money with him this time. I said did he want me to take him there, he said no, as they were going to collect him. I thought it didn't take the massage parlour long to see a new market with collection and delivery included. I was sitting in the restaurant having breakfast when both Janet and Jane asked if they could join me. We have decided to have a good breakfast then we are going to see a friend who lives nearby. They were both enjoying the holiday, and Jane said she had been waiting for someone like me to start providing holidays like this, to do things like everybody else can. They asked me where Albert was, I said, 'Guess.' They looked at each other and laughed, especially when I told them they were going to pick him up, and take him back. I told them we were going to leave for the dinner cruise at 5 p.m. They told me that if they weren't here, to go without them as they may have dinner with their friend.

We were soon loading the coach for our transfer to the docks to join our boat for dinner. The same guide was with us, and she said she had been down to the docks that morning to see the boat and there were no steps. We arrived at the port to a sigh of anguish from the guide. 'What's wrong?' I said. She looked out of the window and pointed to our boat, which was moored and tied to another one. In fact, to get to it we would have to cross six other boats to get onto our boat. We started to unload the coach making our way to the first boat; getting on was no problem as it was level with the ground, we now had to lift the wheelchair over the side onto the next one.

Within minutes, many of the crew appeared, and lifted our clients over the rest of the boats to ours. I was amazed how helpful they were. It was just yet another adventure with many more to come over the future years. We were soon pulling out of the harbour where all you could see were ships moored everywhere—this was such a busy harbour. The meal was a buffet so we took the clients to see what was on offer, and got it for them. It was very good, and everyone enjoyed the night. I even danced with the guide.

The next day after breakfast, it was time to load the coach for our trip to the airport for our flight to Penang, Malaysia. I had all of the tickets and passports, and went straight to the check in desk (can't do this today). This was done very quickly, and we would be called when needed—time for a coffee and chat. We only had one excursion booked in Penang; the rest of the time would be used for relaxing, and enjoying the beautiful weather. We were soon boarding the aircraft, and on our way—for us, this was a short flight—after what we had been used to recently. The airport was small and easy to get around. We soon had our luggage, and we're making our way to customs. Our coach was outside, which we could see from the customs desk. Most of our group had gone through customs, and the driver was loading people on.

I was at the customs decks with Jane and Janet, and they asked to look through her case. As Janet opened Jane's case, on top were all of the unused syringes used to inject her insulin. All of a sudden, many police appeared and surrounded us. 'What are these used for?' said the officer. Janet looked at the officers, and told them it was to inject insulin for Janes diabetes. They wanted to see the insulin, and made a call to the on call doctor so this could be checked. The doctor arrived, checked the insulin, and confirmed what it was and what it was used for. They counted the syringes, and said there were ten; and when we checked in to go home, we were to show we had ten syringes including the used ones to prove we had not sold them. Both Malaysia and Singapore take the smuggling of drugs as a capital offence, and take no excuses. Jane, Janet, and myself were quite shook up about what had happened. I said whatever we, do we can't lose any of those needles.

The hotel was very comfortable, and I was sure the group would enjoy their stay. We had a good dinner, and talked about what to do tomorrow; and it was agreed a day of leisure round the swimming pool, well it wasn't about to turn out that way. The hotel never had a massage parlour, which didn't please Albert. The next day, we all enjoyed a great breakfast, and then sat around the swimming pool. It was a hot day, and I should have been aware of that. Tom and I were helping Albert and Mike in the pool, and getting out of the way of Gwen who had very restricted vision; and although could swim very well, kept hitting the ends of the pool due to the fact that she couldn't see them I tried shouting out to her she was too near the poolside, when you're in the pool helping, you tend to forget how quickly time goes by, and that you are bearing your skin to the very hot sun. Everyone was soon sitting around the tables put together for our group. Swimming does make you hungry, and the food on the menu was looking very appetizing. We all sat around the table enjoying a drink, and the food that was ordered.

After an hour or so, Bob and his friend Bob came, and joined us and let us know that on the beach, they were doing parachute flights over the sea. He asked me if I wanted to see, I said I would join him and see how this was done. What happens is they put the parachute onto you, which is attached to a boat; the boat then heads out to sea getting faster as the person runs along the beach, and gets lifted in the air. That was fine going up but what about coming down. The boat heads toward the beach, and at the last minute turns, which means the person goes straight to the beach and then lands. Bob wanted to go up, and asked if Tom and I could lift him, and run while the parachute filled up with air letting him go as he was lifted. Seemed easy enough!

I went back to the rest of the group to tell them what was about to happen, and yes, they all wanted to come down to watch. Bob went to see the boat driver, and a price of £10.00 was agreed. Someone came over with the parachute, and started fixing it on Bob; he then took the rest down to the boat. Then the two people at the boat signalled to us to lift Bob, Tom, and myself lifted him up, and we then saw the lead being pulled forward as the boat started to speed up, Tom and I were now running down the beach getting nearer the water. I thought any second now we will have to throw him in the air, and I just hope he goes upwards. We did and he fell down toward the beach, and just before he hit the beach, he went shooting at great speed upwards. As he went up, he looked smaller. The rest of the group were amazed at what had just happened as if it were a miracle. Jane and Mike now also wanted to go up, I asked them if they were sure, and they were. Now the hard part was about to begin—that was catching Bob as he comes down. The boat was heading toward the beach—it was time. As the boat turned, it powered down. Bob was heading toward us. We were now running to get underneath him, and he was now dropping quicker. We took the strain, and fell on the beach with him on top of us, but he was unhurt, and so were we. The guy came over and took the parachute off Bob, and it was now being fixed on Mike. Mike can walk, but not run so we once again lifted him and ran. He went up very quickly as he was a lot lighter than Bob. We got Bob back into his wheelchair, and he was just so happy that he had done it. He said he never dreamed he would ever fly by parachute; his face was so happy. Mike was now halfway round so we started to walk back down the beach to catch him knowing he would be a lot easier, and he was. Mike was so excited at what he had just done. He kept shouting it must have been the adrenaline. Jane was brought over, and attached to the parachute. We ran down the beach again, and she was in the air. As she went up, there was a clapping noise from people on the beach who had been watching us. Some came over to us, and said it was a great thing to see. Jane landed, and we were soon sitting round our table by the pool discussing the adventure. Unfortunately, due to the excitement I forgot just how hot it was. When I looked down at my legs and then my arms, I saw how red they had gotten. I looked around the group, and they too were getting a little red.

I took Albert back to our room and went into the shower, which hurt. I thought, *Oh Dear.* That night at dinner, I not only hurt, but started not to feel that good. It looked like sunstroke. Luckily, no one else looked ill—the whole discussion at dinner was the parachute adventure. I went to bed early, as I didn't feel well at all. I asked Tom to take over for me, as I did not know how I would be the next day. I was up and down all night; first, I was boiling hot so I had the air con on full, then I was freezing cold so up went the heat in the room. I must have drunk half a gallon of water. I was half asleep and I could hear Albert grunting and groaning in the background. He had got himself in his wheelchair, and was making his way to the toilet. He looked over and asked how I was. I said, 'Just a bit better, but I didn't want to do much today.'

He looked over and said, 'I hope you're better soon.'

I explained 'One-minute I was baking, and the next I was freezing'

He said, 'really?' I said, of course knowing that was down to me. I stayed in bed most of the day and by the evening was a lot better, enough to go down for dinner, so I could let the group know about the shopping trip tomorrow.

The rest of the holiday went very well, and it wasn't long before I was at the check in desk for a flight to Kuala Lumpur then onto Heathrow. I had the entire luggage lined up, and all the passports. As soon as I gave the passports over, the girl looked through them until she came to Jane's—I knew then what she would do. Sure enough, she went on the phone so I pre-empted her, and called Janet and Jane over. The policeman arrived at the check in so Janet opened up the case, and gave him the broken syringes, and the rest were there for him to count. Soon, we were all checked in, and on our way home. A holiday full of memories and lessons for incoming agents, this was to go on for many years to come and still does now. It was nice to be part of it from the beginning.

CHAPTER 5

How many holidays can we sell? I was asked this in my office as we had a staff meeting just five in our management team. I don't know, as there are so many factors we have to look at. We were sending mail shots to a list of day centres, which were listed in the social service list book. We were getting many requests for day trips and short stay weekends. We also were asked by Granada Studios to look at the facilities for disabled people. As they were going to start new studio tours later that year. Of course, if you are a resident of the UK, you will be aware just how popular Coronation Street is. So they knew many millions of people would visit over the coming years. It was popular, and we ended up taking many thousands of disabled people over the years. This really pleased me as they and others were at last seeing the need for access, and it would create more business, which Granada Studios were now seeing and getting very satisfied customers.

The problem was that both our holidays and day trips—all happened from March to October. Flying holidays of course were no problem, as we could arrange them to fill gaps. They were usually far away holidays, which tended to be more expensive. We found that we had a certain amount of clients who were up for adventure, and loved to travel to far off places they had always wished they could go to. I started to speak to them on the telephone to get their opinion on the holiday and the price so I knew we had a holiday that was going to go. It was the others we had to keep our eye on.

We also used to supply three different care services, which was Bill's idea. We had long since lost the police cadets as we were not a charity but commercial, and had a list we had built up over the last few years. The three different systems were Basic Care: this is when a client could look after themselves; Share Care: when a client needed some help, and one helper would share two clients; Exclusive Care: this is what is says where a client had a helper to themselves. As you can imagine, sometimes the share system gave us problems when one needed more care than the other; so on every holiday, we tried to have at least one floating helper in case of problems. We later changed the system to PAP (personal assistance package). This was done on what the client needed, and would be priced accordingly. Even though on many occasions, this was not always accurate and stretched our staff to the limit. Also, because we were a commercial operation, our insurers didn't like us providing help, and the cost of insurance every year got bigger. I said to Bill that this would have to be looked at as the cost kept on rising. Bill said that we should only start to worry about the cost when the clients who had care stopped coming. I thought, well that's one way of looking at it. There were many clients who had no one to go with them, and without our help, they would not have been able to go. When I looked back many years later, I found that some of the clients we took on holiday that needed our care, and who had some kind of speech problems, actually stopped couples who did not need personal help coming back with us again as they didn't want other people to think they were part of the same group. I told this to other people later, and they were shocked to hear that, but this did happen many times.

As I have said before, planning holidays back in the 1980s was a lot different to now. It was decided to include a Christmas holiday for this year, and to send it out through our mailing list as a flyer to see the response; and if enough booked we would go ahead with it. We had to do this as quickly as we could because Christmas was a busy period, which hoteliers could sell very quickly. In fact, we found many hotels had the same clientele every Christmas due to the repeat bookings every year, which could cause a problem of ever getting a booking in the first place. This was exactly what happened, and it was to be a few more years before our first Christmas holiday was to happen.

We started planning our coach holidays, avoiding dates where we knew we could sell the coach space. We were getting lots of requests sometimes at short notice because people thought it was like booking standard coaches, and when we told them there were none available, some people would get very upset. We tried to tell customers that they should book as much in advance as possible. That way, they would stand a better chance of getting the coach. Potential customers would ask us why is it only your company that have these coaches. I would say I did not know. Many would then say this is not good enough, they should make it law, and they were going to write to their MP. I knew eventually that it would become a law on access as it was political, and at last for disabled people, things were moving forward, but transport would take a long time to recognize the need for access.

I have for many years tried to show coach operators the benefit of having accessible coaches. It means that you can increase your sales as you get access to another market as well as the one you already have. Also, it was to show that disabled didn't mean wheelchair user. Indeed, now as people live longer and longer, they find it harder to climb stairs—especially on coaches. So operators that see this will do better in the future. If you are a coach operator who also run their own holidays, and have a loyal following, you would have done your research and kept your costs under control. Nevertheless, if your loyal clients are having a problem boarding and getting off your coach, they might stop coming with you. Why lose them when you needn't? I was told by one operator that if they put lifts on their coaches, many of their clients would stop coming with them as they thought the holidays would be full of wheelchair users, and they didn't want to go on holiday with them. Unfortunately, that attitude was not unusual then, and believe it or not, some still exists today—although not as much.

I was giving a talk at a coach operator's conference once, and after dinner, I was talking to a large operator who had been providing Coach

Holidays for many years. He agreed with me about the coach hire part of my talk. In that, he would be gaining more business as his coaches could operate in both markets. Nevertheless, he would not take disabled people due to the fact his other clientele would stop coming. I found that hard to believe at the time, but over the years, found he was right; and maybe for many reading this book, you too would find it hard to believe. There are of course reasons for this. Many non-disabled people didn't know how to cope with disabled people. Were they saying the right thing, acting the correct way, because for so long. There had been little, or no interaction with disabled people as they were unable to go where they wanted to as there were no facilities; and now more was happening to make integrated travel happen, I also found that when it comes to people with a mental disability, some disabled clients who would go on our holidays felt very uncomfortable with anyone with a mental disability. I found the most interesting clients the ones that had become disabled in later life, as they knew what it was like before their disability; I have known a few clients, who through accidents, have lost either one or two legs and use a wheelchair now. They see how easy it is sometimes to make things better. I remember a client, who came with us many times, who had lost both legs in an accident. He did like his drink, and most of the time we were together, he had had quite a few as he used to start at ten in the morning. I asked him how long he had been drinking like he did, and he said he couldn't remember, but it helped him through the day.

Worldwide, there seemed to be more and more little companies starting that said they specialized in holidays for the disabled—although there were only a few in Europe. Most were providing group holidays like us, some would soon be looking at individual holidays as soon as there were access rooms and transport. Many charities now had holiday officers, and their job was to see what accessible transport and accommodation there was in a given location. Bill was contacted by RADAR, then called the Royal Association of Disability and Rehabilitation, who wanted to know if we had any information on Israel regarding access. I told Bill we had not, and he explained he had a call from the holiday officer at RADAR; and if possible, could we go and see her. So we set a date and went.

A commercial company and the Israeli tourist board wanted to be able to arrange holidays for disabled people to Israel. They wanted me to help with the transport and Bill for the holiday side. Both Bill and I were pleased to be asked, and accepted their offer. It wasn't long before we were on our way to Ben Gurion Airport with Fiona, the new holidays officer at RADAR. On arrival, we were met by someone from the tourist office, and taken to our hotel in Tel Aviv. Security was very tight, but being with the tourist board helped a bit. We had a meeting that night, and were told about our itinerary for the next few days. The tourist board were very interested in our ideas on access both in transport and accommodation; and arrangements had been made to visit hotels, tourist attractions, and the main bus company. My visit was first the next day.

After breakfast, I waited in the lobby for someone to contact me. Sure enough, right on time he turned up, and we sat for at least over one hour with drawings and photographs. It was a very productive meeting, and over the next few months, liaised together in the building of the bus. I also got involved with the access in accommodation, as by now I knew what was needed; and understanding the commercial side, which had to be looked at. On our way back, we were discussing how good it was to see other countries taking such an interest in access. Bill said that perhaps, one of the reasons was to help its own population, as there were many with some disability due to the troubles at the time.

The way accessible transport can come about has always amazed me. I was working for a company in London that dealt with supplying five-day tours of London for Hungarian people—this was when they were still in the Soviet bloc. The agency was part of the Hungarian government, and brought Hungarians to the UK for holidays ; and hopefully, people from the UK to Hungary. We did many of these trips. None of the clients were disabled, this proved having an accessible coach increased your turnover, and of course profit, as we could do access jobs as well where the others couldn't.

One day, I had a telephone call from the manager of the agency asking about the adaptions on our coaches, and would it be possible to use the lift for people who found it difficult to climb stairs. I said that would be no problem as that is why they are there. He was amazed we had such equipment. A few days later, he asked if I could make time to come up to see him at his office. I agreed, and went a few days later. He told me that he had been speaking to his superiors in Budapest, and they were very interested in having a coach like mine for tourists coming to Hungary; and maybe I would be interested in sending clients, and helping to promote travel to Hungary. I said I was always interested in promoting access anywhere. A few days later, Gabor, the manager of the agency contacted me. He asked for dates that I could go out to Budapest, and meet with people in the bus factory to help with their design. He asked for my passport so he could put the visa in it, and a few days later, I was off to Budapest. I was met at the airport by someone from the bus factory who took me to my hotel, which was on St Margaret's island in the river Danube. So here I was in a communist country, a place I never thought I would be in, and all because of accessibility. It really was amazing.

The man from the factory told me he would be here at 6 a.m. They didn't waste time out there then, and sure enough, he was here dead on time. I got into his car, and we went off through Budapest—a very interesting city. I was taken aback by the amount of people standing at the tram and bus stops, and they stood all in line, no one pushing, all dressed much alike. We arrived at the factory, and went into the canteen where there were another six people waiting around a table. We all made our introductions, and breakfast was served during which as you can imagine, I was asked many questions about why I went into this business. I also asked them why they were interested in this market, and to be honest, it was the last business I would have expected them to go into. I think they found my attitude somewhat strange, and of course, now I can understand why as I have been to Budapest many time since they left the communist bloc.

We had a successful few days, and I was to use the coach on many a holiday which I would send to Hungary in the future—events were becoming very interesting. All of a sudden, people from other countries were also looking at a new potential travel market, but they had to understand it was made up of different sections. Even to the new Paralympics, which was started by Stoke Mandeville Hospital near Aylesbury. Because they had heard about our coaches, we were asked to collect worldwide athletes from both Heathrow and Gatwick airports. They were very surprised when they saw our coaches as they expected to struggle up the stairs, which normally happened. I was so pleased to hear their comments because once again it proved once more what simple transport access would achieve worldwide.

There were people who wanted to travel alone but needed help, and others that wanted to join group holidays. Operating coach group tours like me found it difficult to find hotels with many accessible rooms at that time, and still do for groups, but the individual market would not really take off until there was more accessible transport for airport transfers and excursions. This was to take many years, and it is just happening now. The more access there is, the better it will become. In the future, there will no longer be the need for specialized travel companies dealing with disabled people. Everyone including wheelchairs will be able to travel on coach holidays; there won't be a situation where people are separated due to access. However, this will still take time, and there will still be the growing number of providers for holidays for disabled people only.

CHAPTER 6

I woke up with a start as drinks were being served with sandwiches. I thought, not long to land now the hard work was about to begin. Once again, Albert wanted lifting up as he had moved halfway down the seat whist he was asleep. I got the holiday file out of my briefcase, which was up in the overhead lockers. I looked at the clients that had requested carry on/off to their wheelchairs, everything was correct none of them could walk and would need the carry chair. I asked the chief steward how long before landing (thinking of toilets), and he said at least three hours so there was no panic. I was enjoying my coffee and sandwiches remembering the amount of times sitting on the aircraft getting ready to land thinking of the different countries, and sometimes the problems it could cause you; and of course, the clients—so many of them—and how so many were so excited at landing at an airport they never thought they would. I was with our first group to Hawaii, everyone was so excited, and I had many return clients on this trip so I knew most of them quite well. The flight had been from Gatwick with Air New Zealand via Los Angeles where we changed planes and were now heading to Honolulu. I had been there a few years before, and found its accessibility first class. It also had accessible transport all be it in smaller vehicles, which made having only one guide for the three vehicles a somewhat challenging exercise, and a worn out guide at the end of it.

I had arranged some good excursions including one to the big island Hawaii where Captain Cook met his end, and of course why the Union Jack is still in the corner of the Hawaiian flag. As you can imagine, the flight was a long one, and we had a few smokers including me on board. Although most of us coped including me, I had one client who wanted to light up as he found it really hard. I said to him that they are very strict, and he could be arrested when we landed. It really was best to wait, and I would be the first to join him when we got outside the airport. John liked a drink as well as a cigarette. It seemed an age for me but a lifetime for John, the plane soon landed, and we were soon off the aircraft on our way to immigration and customs.

Because of the location of Honolulu, an island in the Pacific Ocean, you tend to forget it is part of the United States. We collected the luggage, and I had found out where the vehicles should be waiting so we made our way round. Like most times in Hawaii, it was a beautiful evening, and both John and I were enjoying a well- anticipated cigarette—my god, it was good. I could see two of the vehicles, and they said the other one was on its way. You can guess who said he would wait for the third one, as he must have been on his tenth cigarette by now. Although the clients were tired, they were just amazed at the views and the place itself; and having stayed at the hotel, I knew they would be really over the moon, and they certainly were. Both Denis and Tom were with me on the tour, and once we checked in, they were taking the clients up to their rooms, and I told them I would meet them in the bar. Apart from me, no one had ever been to Honolulu before, so I spent an hour talking to both Denis and Tom about what there was local, and the excursions we were going on. I had arranged a breakfast meeting in a room off of the restaurant so I could tell the clients what the programme was, and of course what was to see locally.

I got down to the restaurant at about 9.30. Both Denis and Tom were there, Denis was looking after John, and he wanted room service, as he didn't go out very much. Gradually, the rest of the clients were arriving at the restaurant, and taking advantage of the fantastic things that were on offer. They were so impressed with the hotel, and you could see they were very happy with the food on offer too. I gave them about thirty minutes, then got up to tell them about where they were and its history. I gave out some itineraries, which I had made out a few weeks before the holiday, which showed times on the excursions. After I had gone through our programme, I think they were ready to start exploring Waikiki. I told them I would see them tomorrow for our tour of Pearl Harbour. I asked Albert what he wanted to do, and he said he didn't mind, so we walked along by the beach overlooking the Pacific Ocean. Albert was always a fan of Hawaii Five O, and I knew where they had filmed the opening shots so I took him down to where their headquarters were to see if he recognized it, which he did. He said, 'When I see a repeat of this, I will always remember this spot and this day.'

I was walking back with Albert when I saw Denis coming out of a shop with a bag of spirits. He looked over at us, and as he laughed, he said, 'This will be my daily exercise collecting John's drinks and cigs.' He was correct because all the time we were in the hotel, he never went out. He would eat, drink, and smoke on his balcony; in fact, one day he dropped a cigarette on the carpet, and burnt a large hole in it. 'That's why I have travel insurance,' he said.

The next day was here before we knew it, and I was waiting for the mini coaches for our trip to Pearl Harbour. All three arrived, and we started loading. It was as usual a wonderful day in paradise. We arrived at the harbour, and went into the visitors waiting area because it was from here we would be loaded on a boat to be taken to the memorial platform built over the Arizona ship that was sunk during the raid in December 1941. The strange thing that has always surprised me is the fact that the majority of visitors are Japanese, something you wouldn't think of; as they were the ones that attacked it.

Everyone enjoyed the trip. A client said to me Pearl Harbour is a name everyone has heard of, so it is very nice to have been there. On our way back to the hotel, I could hear some of the clients talking about the war, and some were talking about the bombing of London. It reminded me of a holiday in Wales where for some reason all my clients were much older than average, and all had war memories.

I was looking after a man who was in his '90s, and who had been a navigator in a Mosquito Bomber during the war. He used a wheelchair, as he couldn't walk any distance. He was a very interesting man to talk to; and although he was in his '90s, he still loved the ladies, and told me of his wartime conquests. Indeed, we were on an excursion one day so I asked him if he would like a tea in one of the tea rooms, and he said no and could I park him in an area a few yards away. So in his words, he could watch all the old girls getting off the coaches and buses.

There was another lady who had hired an electric scooter, which had been delivered to the hotel. I took it to the lady concerned, and showed her how to charge it. It was then I found out she had never been on one before, and had no idea how to drive it. So I took her to the esplanade by the beach, and spent a few hours with her. I was still concerned however; and sure enough after I had parked up my man on the excursion, she came along at full speed, and hit a table outside a tea room tipping it over will an almighty crash. Luckily enough, no one was at the table at the time. I asked one of my staff to keep an eye where possible. Another lady once again in her '90s—she had a foreign accent—I asked her where she was born. My dear she said, 'I was born in Austria, but I have been in England all the years since the war.'

I said, 'So you were in Austria in the war.'

'Oh yes,' she said. 'In fact, I was in the Hitler youth.' She looked around to see if anyone else was listening, 'We did not know how bad Hitler was. We were told he was a good leader. There wasn't newspapers and television then.' She looked around again, she got closer to me, 'One day,' she said, 'I was at a rally, and Hitler was in his car, which stopped near me. He got out and walked towards me, and put his hand on my shoulder, and I looked into his very blue eyes.'

I said, 'You met Hitler!' 'Yes, and the rest of them.'

I thought this lady is living history. I said, 'How did you end up in England?'

'After the war,' she said. 'People had to report to either the English or the American camp. I had learned English so went to the English one. Whilst I was there, someone came over to me, and he asked if

I wanted a job as my English was so good. That was the man that I married, and came over to England with. I then found out he worked for MI6.'

I thought you could not make this up, what a story. The man I was looking after loved this story as well. He told me that one of the worse jobs he did when flying was taking spies to parachute into the occupied country to carry out their job. He said they were mainly young girls, and he would help them when the bomb doors opened. He said he would hold their hands, and look into their eyes, which were full of fear. They were about to drop into the darkness into an occupied country where if they were caught, they would be tortured and killed. 'I never saw any of them again unsung heroes,' he said.

Every one of the clients had a story to tell, which I found fascinating. I love History, and this was something else. He told me that sometimes, he felt guilty. Because of his job, he really did not ever go hungry, and also never went short of alcohol as he was also on active flying. He told me that he was also a dancing teacher, which he did for many years. I said to him, 'I think I know why you wanted to do this, was it that you were always in the company of women?'

'You can see right through me,' he said.

One night in the hotel, there was a hen night, so many young girls around. I was sitting in the bar with my man, and he was studying all the girls over the night. After a few hours, he whispered in my ear, 'See that one in the green?'

I said, 'Yes.'

He said, 'She's ripe now.' He looked at me and smiled.

I thought if he is like this at his age, I have many more years yet thank goodness. Another client, sitting around the dinner table one night, said that she and her husband were married in early 1939, and they had a honeymoon she said she would always remember. Of course later that year, war was declared and her husband was sent off, and never come back; and even to this day, there was a small tear in her eye when she thinks of him.

What was very interesting about this group of clients was that they needed help and access because of their age, not their disability.

These clients could have gone with any other holiday company, but they chose us because of the access explained in our brochure. One thing I have learned from doing this job is how the second world war affects people so differently. It really gives you an understanding of people, especially when you combine this knowledge with how disability had been treated from the war until now. I remember telling a friend of mine the stories told to me by these people, and he said imagine what a fantastic film this would make with flashbacks on all the clients during the war. I thought he really had a point.

We had spent a very enjoyable two weeks in paradise, and now the long flight from Honolulu to Gatwick. I remember the fight from Honolulu a few years before going the other way to Auckland, New Zealand. This is a long flight that lands in Auckland at approximately 8 a.m., and was a real problem when we arrived. The holiday then was an ambitious project that had never been done before over such a distance. It all started when I was approached by someone from our tourist board to see if a coach operator from New Zealand could come and see our accessible coaches. I was shocked that an operator halfway around the world is interested when operators in the UK were not.

A couple of weeks later, I met some people from New Zealand accompanied by two people from our tourist board. It was a really great meeting, and I asked if there were any tour operators in NZ who did the same as me. No was the answer, but the coach operator said they were looking for people like me to send clients over, as they believed NZ had a lot to offer people with disabilities. We had a great lunch together in a real English pub next to my garage where we talked about the future of disabled travel, and how glad I was that there was going to be a coach available in NZ later that year. They also told me of a good travel agent in London who was the main supplier of air tickets from the national airline, Air New Zealand. Apparently, he also run in conjunction with our ministry of agriculture trips around our farms for NZ farmers, so he might be looking for coach hire. I thought this business is all about contacts. The NZ coach operator asked if he could contact me if he had problems with the coach conversion. I said not a problem, but to remember the twelve-hour time difference.

A few days later, I got a call from the travel agent whom had been contacted by our tourist board. He said if I had time, maybe it would be a good idea if I could come up to London to meet with him at his office just off Oxford street. A few days later, I was on the tube making my way to his office. When I arrived, I met Philip; and it's one of those things in life that you know you are going to get on, and we certainly did, and Phil was to become a good friend of mine. He thought my idea was good, and the more people from main street tourism that got involved, the better. He also asked about our coaches, which I showed him pictures of. He gave me a package with a farming tour arranged for later that year so I could quote on it. We started to discuss flights with air NZ of which he was their biggest agent in the UK. He suggested that due to the length of the flights, it may be a good idea we stopped off at LA coming back, and Honolulu going out. I agreed with him, and asked if he would make out an itinerary for NZ as he had been their many times before, and I would do Honolulu and LA.

This would be an ambitious project due to the distance and countries involved, and had never been done before for disabled people. It took a month to put this together, and although I trusted Phil with the route and excursions in NZ, I also contacted the hotels myself to make sure there was as much access as possible. I had a list of eighteen names—one of them was Albert. The rest of the group had their own helpers, so our company did not have to supply anyone but me to run the tour. Daunting thought on your own, and having Albert to look after! Phil had booked the air seats, and advised me to go to their office in Hammersmith to meet them; and also, to make sure the seats were locked into the system due to the amount of flight legs there would be. At that time, it would be Gatwick/LA, LA/Honolulu, Honolulu/Auckland, Auckland/Christchurch, Auckland/LA, LA/Gatwick. The people I met at ANZ were all very helpful, and fully understood the reasons why people had to sit where they were planned due to them being family; and also, so they could get to the toilet as easy as possible and to make their journey as comfortable as possible, as they would able - bodied passengers, or they should do.

The last couple had arrived so we all went over to the ANZ check in desk for the first flight going to LA. The check in was fine, and we were soon at the gate loading the aircraft, and climbing over northern England on our way. The flight seemed to go very quickly, and we were soon on our descent into LA International. After everyone else got off, we were transferred to a waiting aircraft by a very efficient crew into our pre-arranged seats. We then had a five-hour flight to Honolulu—if it could only be like this all the time!

The Hawaii adventure would have gone very well apart from a problem caused by me. We got to the hotel in the early hours of the morning, and as I got out of the mini coach. I slipped, and fell on my foot. The pain was excruciating, and I had to check in the group before I could do anything more. I hobbled up pushing Albert's chair, which actually helped, to our room where I collapsed on the bed and looked at my foot. It was black by bruising. Albert came out of the toilet, and looked over at my foot. 'Bloody hell, son,' he said. 'Hope you ain't broke it.'

'So do I,' said I, touching my foot tenderly.

I thought I would try and get some sleep, and see what it was like later. I woke up in the morning, and it was very painful. I thought I have no option, but to have it seen to. Luckily today, it was free, and we were meeting at the breakfast bar so I could go through our itinerary whilst here. I got Albert down to the breakfast area where the rest of the group were. Everyone was concerned. I told them not to worry, as I had already found out there was a doctor on call in the hotel, and I had made an appointment at reception. Two of our clients, Jane and Andrew, were to be a big help to me. Jane worked at a care home where Andrew was a resident, and was asked if she would accompany him on this fabulous holiday, as there was no one else to accompany him. I knew I had to go up to the thirtieth floor where the doctor was, so asked Albert if I could use his chair, as I could then get up there without so much pain. I pushed Albert out to the swimming pool where there was waiter service so knew he would be okay. He got out of his chair, and sat round the table. As I got into his chair, Jane and

Andrew came over, and she asked if I wanted a push up to the doctor. I said, 'Are you sure? Andrew will be okay?'

'Oh, yes,' she said. 'I am sure Albert will keep an eye on him,' Albert looked up and laughed, and then looked at Jane and said,

'And don't you be too long.'

The hotel we were in was large. It had over thirty disabled rooms, and was on thirty-third floor. Jane pushed me into the lift, and we went up to the thirtieth floor where when we got out, it was assigned to the doctor. Jane pushed me in, and the nurse who was British came over to take my details, I thanked Jane, and asked her if she would keep an eye on Albert. The nurse asked me how it had happened, and what my job was. I told her my fear about it being broken, and asked her for her opinion. She said, 'Until we see the x- ray, I can't tell.'

'Can you do the x-ray here?'

'Oh, yes,' she said. 'That's where I am going to take you now.'

I had the x-ray, and waited in a nice room with coffee, tea, etc. The nurse came over, and pushed me into the doctor's room. He was looking at the x-ray, and he looked over at me and said, 'Well, it's not broken, but it will damage your foot if you keep on walking on it.'

I said to him that I had seventeen days in NZ, and four in LA to do yet, and these people need my help. 'Is there any way you could take the pain away?'

He looked at me and said, 'I have some tables I can give you, and although it would help with your walking, you might find it could damage your foot. When you get back to England, you must go to your doctor, and show him these pills so he can examine your foot. If you agree, this I will give you the tablets.'

'Of course,' I agreed, and he gave me enough tablets to carry on with the tour. I took the first one of two a day, and wheeled myself back to the pool. I got back to the pool where Albert was talking to other members of our holiday. They all asked how I was, and were pleased I could continue. For the next few hours, I sat around the table talking to some of our clients about how disabled holidays were growing; and if it weren't for them, progress would not happen. All of a sudden, the pain started to leave my foot. I put it to the ground, and stood up—all seemed fine. I was relieved, and felt a lot happier. It was time for Albert to buy me a drink.

It was an evening check in for our flight from Honolulu to Auckland. My foot was fine as I have got to know when to take the tablet to avoid the pain. We will be arriving at approximately 8 a.m. NZ time, then go through the usual arrival checks before finding out where the domestic airport is for our flight to Christchurch. *Should be okay*, I thought.

I have learned to get as much sleep as you can on a flight, and did on this one so I felt fine as I was eating breakfast and getting ready to land. We were soon on our descent into Auckland, and had pulled up on the pier when it was announced that there was a strike at the airport—there were no porters, and other type of staff. I thought they must have known but tell me now. I asked the steward what that would mean for us, he said he didn't know exactly at the moment. As the other passengers were getting off, I saw our wheelchairs were arriving. *One good thing*, I thought. Mind you, there was no one around to push. Luckily enough, with me pushing Albert, we could cope so we headed for immigration, which was straightforward then to luggage. Now this was going to be a problem, but I forgot that had been sent to the domestic flight. I was shown where we would get the bus to the domestic terminal. The vehicle arrived, which was a large bus with no lift (no one had told me this) so everyone had to be lifted on by the driver and myself (bad foot as well). I wasn't happy, let alone the clients. It took only ten minutes to get to the domestic terminal where all had to be got off. We then made our way to check in for our next flight.

The clients could see I was not happy after the transfer episode, and the fact there was a strike. We were checked in, and soon started to load the aircraft. I knew that at least when we got to Christchurch, the coach would be accessible for the rest of the NZ part of the holiday. We were soon in the air and on our way.

The light lunch was going down well, and my foot was fine—bloody good tablets these. I asked one of the stewards if there was a strike at Christchurch airport, and they confirmed there wasn't. I sat back and thought, thank god for that. It shouldn't take long to get out of the airport as this was a domestic flight, and we had already done all the checks. All we needed was the luggage (that was not going to be that easy) the aircraft landed, and taxied to the terminal. People got off the aircraft, and I was waiting by the door for our wheelchairs. Some people arrived with airport chairs, I asked where ours were, and they said they didn't know. They were just told to get up to the aircraft to get us off. We were soon off the aircraft, and down by the luggage carousel. I got the entire luggage onto an airport cart, and we went through into the terminal. I saw the coach driver as he held a board with Chalfont line on it. I went over to the ANZ desk to find out about our wheelchairs. Someone came over, and I could tell by her face something was up. She said, 'I am so sorry, but your wheelchairs were not loaded and are still in Auckland, but they would be on the next flight which would arrive in four hours.'

I could see the clients were really pissed off by now, and we all just wanted a rest. Also, my foot was starting to hurt. I called over the driver and asked him how far in time was the hotel from the airport. He said approximately thirty to forty-five minutes. I went over to the ANZ desk, and said that we were not prepared to wait hours in the terminal even with a free lunch, which they had offered. It was their fault so I was going to our hotel, and when our chairs arrived, they should send them to our hotel where they could pick theirs up. They didn't want to do this. I said, 'Really, you have no choice. You didn't load their chairs. It's your fault. Why should we be held up? You will just have to be more careful in the future.'

I told the driver to push Albert, and to escort the group to the coach, and I would bring over the luggage. The coach was nearly an exact copy of mine in the UK, so I was pleased to see clients going up on the lift and being able to travel in eventually, their wheelchair. I thought I don't want to see an airport now for the next sixteen days. It took another six hours before our chairs turned up, so I was so glad I took the decision I did.

The next sixteen days went very well, and all my clients had a fantastic time. I am sure a few would love to have moved out there if they had the chance to. So far, the checking in had been fine as all our seats had been locked into the computer system. You can guess what is now about to happen. It was an evening check in at Auckland. I arrived at the check in desk with our tickets, and they started to print out the boarding passes. To my horror, some of them had the wrong seat number on them. I asked the person on the check in why this was happening. I showed him a letter from London why and how we had these seats on all of the legs booked. He said someone must have opened up the booking to move some about, to fit other passengers in. I said I was not happy, and these would have to be put back. The two people on the desk worked very hard, and managed to get them all back, which of course now had moved other passengers around. The manager said to me that because someone had got into the system, it would cause a problem on my return from LA.

On arrival in LA, it was a hectic schedule, with Universal Studios and The first Disney Park, Disneyland. Then we were off back to the UK. The day of the check in arrived, and sure enough, all the seats had been changed. This time, it was more serious as the flight had come from Auckland, and the aircraft already contained passengers bound for Gatwick. I explained once again about how important it was that we have the seats that were booked months ago. The person doing our check in was very rude, and basically ignoring me. All they were doing was just trying to get rid of us. Well, I thought, not me. I had spent a lot of time getting these seats for a reason. I thought, what can I do here? I looked around and thought, I know I will sit on the scales so everything comes to a stop. I did this, and the woman doing the check in told me to get off of the scales or she would tell security. I told her I wanted my seats as ordered. The next thing, a police officer had made his way over. I told him the reason I was there, and she said my seats were not available. He told me to get off the scales or he would arrest me. I put my hands up to him for cuffing and said, 'You arrest me, and you can take care of those people over there, and I will make sure there is a diplomatic incident caused here. I want my seats for my clients who need them.'

He looked over at the clients, and me, then looked up at the women and said in a somewhat John Wayne accent, 'Give him his seats.'

This she did, having to move many who were seated. It was their fault and they should pay. When we arrived back into Gatwick, the ANZ manager was there to meet us to apologize. I said I would be in touch with their head office in Hammersmith. I got home with a very painful foot, and only two tablets left. The next week was unbelievably painful. I went to the doctor, and showed him the pill box, and of course, my foot. He said, 'Where on earth did you got these tablets?' He said they are illegal here. He looked at my foot, and told me I had done a fair bit of damage, and it would take at least a couple of months for it to recover. But I had no option at the time. I am glad to say ANZ sorted out what happened, and two people were sacked—one was the rude woman in LA—and I was so pleased, I wrote to all the clients and let them know.

The plane was now on its descent into Orlando International, another fabulous well-proven holiday was about to begin. I looked out of the window to see the ground looming up, then a bump and the jets screaming as the plane slows down, and leaves the runway.

Soon, we stop at the gate; and I sat and watch as people get up, and start taking things from the overhead lockers. Although it occurs, every flight, this seems to take forever for the passengers to leave the plane. I walk up to the front of the plane to see if our wheelchairs have arrived, and sure enough, they were arriving with the staff from special services. I spoke to the person in charge who I have met before, and he assures me everything is going to plan with no hold ups. And sure enough, soon we were on a good access-able coach on our way to the hotel knowing the next day is a free day. Time to get to know our new clients, maybe around the swimming pool.

CHAPTER 7

Flying is something I have always loved to do, and indeed, my older son liked it so much he is an air steward with British Airways. Unfortunately, it is also a form of transport that is very vulnerable to terrorist attack, which means it is not as easy as it was to fly. When travelling with a group, the tour manager has a great deal of responsibility to cope with, and makes travelling by air harder for all concerned. When it comes to people with disabilities, your knowledge has to include manual and electric wheelchairs, as airport staff can sometimes cause damage to them. I learned everything there is to know about wheelchairs, manual and electric, within a few months of doing this job. You had no other choice, and clients expected you to know how to fix them.

I got to enjoy and look forward to holidays in the UK, as there were no airport problems; and from the start of a coach holiday, it was easy, and everyone who wanted to stay in their wheelchair could and did. There were also no time changes, and the money was the good old pound. We have done many holidays in Devon, I myself, over thirty to forty of them. It was a great week as the excursions were well tried and tested, and none of them were rushed; and of course, when the weather was good, where else would you rather be? Devon also attracted many regular clients, and sometime it was just like a reunion holiday. The hotel we used was a family run hotel, and although it didn't have specific access rooms, the ones we used were okay. We would usually aim for a holiday in late June and September, as they had many families during the school holidays. We would leave London at approximately 12 mid-day, which was also a great benefit as it gave clients more time to get to our London pick up; and of course the same to the other pick-ups on route, but more importantly, there were no security checks—just straight onto the coach. We were then in charge when we wanted to stop and where. I remember one particular Devon trip very well because of some of the clients on it and what happened.

On this holiday, we also had a couple of American clients with their own companions. One of our other clients had bedsores so we had arranged through the NHS for a district nurse to come out a few times during the week we were there. Another one of our regulars, Ron unbeknown to us, had badly scalded his hand and arm. He was a wheelchair user, and had a slight mental disability, and he loved to laugh and be part of all that was going on. He lived on his own, but had people that would come in daily. He would look forward every year to his holiday in Devon, and sometimes would go on another holiday as well. He had a loud voice so everyone near would know what he was saying. He also had a voice that was a little gruff. I was sitting on the same table as Ron when I noticed his hand and forearm. I asked him when he did it, he said the other day. I said that there was a nurse coming in the next day to see another client and would he mind if she had a look at his hand, he said okay very loudly. The next day, Marian saw the nurse, and asked her if she would mind looking at Ron's hand. Marian took her to his room. I was outside the reception having a drink with our new American client when Marian found me, and told me that his hand was in a bad way; and he must have been in pain, and that when she comes back she would dress it again. As she was talking to me, Ron appeared and came over to the table where I was with Brad. 'Ron,' I said. 'How's your hand, does it feel better?'

'Yes,' he said.

'It must have been painful. You make sure you don't bang it.' He looked at me.

'No,' he said. 'She's good.' 'You mean the nurse?' 'Yes,' he said. 'How did you do that, Ron?'

'Well, err I was making a cup a tea, and as I was putting the water in the tea pot, and err the doorbell rang, and it made me jump and the water went over my arm and hand.'

'Bloody hell, Ron! What did she want anyway?' 'Err, to see if I was alright.'

Well, Brad burst into laughter, and Ron sat there looking at him. He then turned to me and said, 'What's he laughing at?'

'Ron, Ron,' I said. 'If only you knew.'

It was being able to use our coaches that made it better for all concerned; and when flying to other countries, you could only go there if indeed they had a coach. We were getting a lot more requests for Scandinavian countries, but after making many enquiries, there was no coach to hire there. Also, there was another problem at that time as the ferries did not have wheelchair- accessible cabins then, and you had to overnight as well. So the only way to do this was to send our coach over empty on the ferry a few days before, and then for it to pick us up at the airport to start our tour. This did make the tour more expensive, but at the time we had no other option. We started to research the tour, and it was decided that we would fly from Heathrow to Gothenburg where the coach would meet us after staying overnight in the hotel that we would stay in for two nights. We would then hire a guide for our journey down to the capital Stockholm where we would use a ferry that we found out had a few more accessible cabins and larger non-access cabins. By no way perfect, but things were beginning to change. I then went to London to visit someone from the Finnish tourist board who I had made contact with a few weeks before. I had told her that I would have a group of about twenty-five pax of which seven would be wheelchair users. She said that she had done some research on where there were suitable rooms, as at that time, once again access rooms were only just being built. All things were booked, and it was put into our next brochure.

It was time to start the holiday, where did the time go from the planning? One of our vehicles picked Marian and I up for our short journey to Heathrow. On arrival, I telephoned one of our helpers Denis, as I knew he was always the first at the airport; and sure enough, he was there. We had sent Denis a list so when we met him, we knew who was there. We were soon checking in and on our way. On landing, we gathered up the luggage, making our way to our coach knowing that loading would be no problem whatsoever.

The hotel was of a good standard, and we were soon checked in. I telephoned the guide to confirm the times for the next day for our tour of Gothenburg. The next day after breakfast, we loaded the coach, and the guide was showing me on her map where we were going. She said she knew the area well, and had made a point of checking it was fine for wheelchairs. I thought, so far so good, but would it last? The answer was *yes* it did. It was a great excursion and well researched. I thanked the guide, and told her we were looking forward to our journey to Stockholm, which she was accompanying us then getting the train back to Gothenburg. We took a nice steady drive to Stockholm, and with the guide, learned a lot about Sweden. We stopped for a nice lunch, leaving enough time for a short tour of Stockholm before dropping off the guide at the station, and making our way to the ferry to Helsinki, Finland. This ferry did have just a few accessible cabins where we were able to put the clients who really needed them. Although I knew a few of the clients, there were some new ones on this trip.

I was looking forward to getting to Helsinki, as another new client would be joining us from Switzerland. All the arrangements had been made by her brother, and she needed some help with her travel in the coach, which we would find out. The trip across was very interesting, and the ferry was very comfortable with excellent food. After breakfast, we loaded the coach, and pulled around to the railway station where we met our guide for the Finland section. Her English was not very good but she had a nice personality. She then took us on a tour of the capital for the next few hours. As usual, every time we stopped and unloaded the coach, many people would stop and watch as it was still quite a unique sight then. We then made our way to our city hotel for one night. We were soon unloaded and in the hotel; and because its location was in the city, many of the clients went out in the afternoon. I stayed in the hotel, as the woman from Switzerland would be arriving at approximately 5 to 5.30.

I saw a cab pull up outside, and went out to look. Yes, it was her. I asked Maureen to give me a hand as she would be looking after her. We both went out, and greeted her, took her up to the room, and I invited her for coffee later after she had unpacked—Maureen stayed with her to help. Her name was Connie, and after twenty minutes or so, they both came into the lounge. Connie was able to propel herself, and had done so for many years so she did not need much help. I asked Connie how she had heard about us, and she told me that if was in a publication to do with her disability, and she had asked her brother to find out about us. She said, 'You do realize you're the only company that provides this type of holiday, and I have been trying to find someone like you for years. They must be very proud of you in the UK.'

I said, 'Connie, I haven't given it a thought. I do this because I enjoy it, and it makes money.'

She said she had seen the coach outside and was impressed, and she had a strange request. I looked at her, and said what that might be. 'Well,' she said. 'When I am sitting up, after a while I get terrible backache. So when I come home in my chair, I have to lie down, as that is the only way the pain will go. So when I am in the coach, can you arrange for me to lie down on the floor on top of the mattresses I have in my case upstairs?'

I said, 'Connie, I can arrange this for you, but all you're going to see is the roof of the coach for the next week and a half.'

I shouldn't have, but I was laughing because you couldn't make this up. Travel from Switzerland to Finland, and tour the country looking at a coach roof. Then she started to laugh, 'I can see the funny side,' she said. 'But it really, it's true.'

I said, 'Your wish is my command, so let's have another coffee.'

The next morning, we started loading the coach making sure no one run Connie over on the floor. Actually, as it turned out, she was very safe and said she was also very comfortable. We started to make our way out of the city, and into the country. The guide was doing her best to explain to us everything in English, and of course, also direct the driver who ended up understanding her sign language better. Over the next week and a half, I lost count of wrong roads we were sent down.

When you talk to suppliers in the travel trade—whether they are commercial or tourist offices—in these early days of providing holidays for disabled people, although I would go out of my way to explain that we don't want any special treatment just the same as anyone else, but to make sure it is accessible if they were a wheelchair user. Some or most would sometimes tend to treat our clients as if they had some sort of intelligence problems. It wasn't their fault, they just wanted to help, but these were just people with a mobility problem. As time went on, of course this started to change, but I can still find this in some places still. The reason why I have put this in the book is because this had a bearing on the accommodation we were about to experience in the next week or so.

Our second day had been interesting. Seeing for the first time, all the people on the coach as well as, the countryside of Finland. We were now heading for our next hotel where we would be based for the next two nights. I don't think the guide had been there before as we kept stopping for her to ask directions. We seemed to be getting further and further into the countryside until a very large building started to appear. As we got closer, I could see ambulances parked in a bay outside; also, there were people outside—some in wheelchairs, others sitting upright on a stretcher smoking cigarettes. They were all in their pyjamas. We come to a stop, and thought where the hell are we. I said to the guide was she sure this was the hotel. She nodded, and pointed to the name on her sheet. I got out and followed her in. Everyone was in uniform—nurses and doctors. I could see no reception desk, and this was a hospital not a hotel. My god, how do I explain this? I thought to myself. I said to the so-called receptionist if I could go and look at a room, she gave me the key. By this, time people were starting to get off the coach. I said to Marian it would be better if people could stay on the coach, but we could unload the luggage from the boot.

A nurse led me to the room I had the key for. I said to her, 'Was this a hospital?'

She had much better English than the guide and replied, 'Yes and no.' She said, 'Some of it was a local hospital, and some a rehab centre.'

And because we had wheelchairs, and were travelling the country, it was only rehab we could stay in as they were the only places with access. This was not explained to me, but I was here now. We walked into the room, which was massive and certainly accessible— there would be no problem with that here. She showed me the rest, which were mainly all the same. Now the hard part, back to the coach to unload and get them to their wards—sorry I mean rooms. I got back to the coach, and it was a hive of activity. The luggage was off onto trolleys, and Tom had started to unload the wheelchairs, which as normal had created people to look at the process. I asked Marian to hand out the keys, and tell everyone to meet in the restaurant in an hour's time. It was easy to find, just follow the knife and fork sign. I went to my room, and started to hang up some clothes from the suitcase; and by the time Marian arrived, I had unpacked most of our clothes. I asked Marian what they thought of the rooms. She smiled and said, 'Not a lot.' I thought maybe the shock was just sinking in.

Twenty minutes to go before we met in the dining room, I said to Marian, 'I will make my way there. Hope to see you there in one piece.'

I was following the sign and walked into. What, looked like a canteen, but it wasn't. Wow, that's a relief, I thought. Two clients then appeared, and walked into the dining room. I looked at them, and they looked back at me. 'Good evening,' I said. 'Everything okay?'

'Well,' said one. 'I have never seen a bathroom so well-equipped, it's really marvellous.'

I couldn't believe what I was hearing, but was going to make the most of it. 'Well,' I said. 'It may be a bit clinical, but this is how they cope with groups with wheelchair clients here.'

'Well, I hope it's all like this,' she said.

'Do we just sit down or pick what we want?' I said. I would find out how they served the dinner here. It was as I thought selfservice, I said to the clients who had arrived, 'Just take what you want, but unlike other people that come in, you don't have to go to the till.'

The food was fine, but nothing to write home about. The guide came over, and sat on my table with Marian and Tom (the driver). Tom was trying to explain to her that he needed to know much sooner about having to make turns, as the coach was over forty feet long; and so far on this tour, he had done more miles backward than forward, but at least the clients sometime saw things twice. I also told her that we needed more explanation of what the history was, and what was going on now in different towns. I found in some instances that a few guides in lots of countries (including the UK) tended to be very cautious in the way they spoke to disabled people. Some even spoke slower, which was terrible. It was just that they had not done this before, and knew nothing about disability. Well, why should they? I doubt if they had seen any before as most people with a disability years ago went with charities.

The rest of the tour went fine as the hospitals become more like hotels as we got nearer Helsinki for our ferry back to Stockholm, then our drive to the airport onto London. I had some very nice letters from clients who really enjoyed the holiday. Many said that they had always wanted to see Finland and Sweden, and were amazed and thought they would never experience nearly twenty- four-hour daylight. Over the years, you get to know many clients personally as you meet them, and run the holiday they are on. You also get a kind of following with the clients who want to see and experience the many things they thought they never would. Many would ask me about different countries, and if it had transport and access. I used to spend many hours talking, and writing plans of their ideas. I would use these ideas later when planning a tour. It was funny that when I was planning, I could see the clients that would want to go, and even funnier, I was usually correct.

From idea to completion, it could take anything from one to six months to plan some tours, as there were so many things to remember and plan for. If it was in Europe, and they had no coach, we would use ours. If by any chance they did have one, I would want to seepictures of it, and also how they would secure the wheelchairs. The UK had the most accessible vehicles, and still has. People now were beginning to take notice that disabled people were a viable market, and one to look at. More hotels were coming on stream with sort of accessible rooms. The problem was who was advising them on access. Over the years, many charitable groups would come up with ideas on how hotel chains should build access room in the hotels; and of course, how many there should be. Unfortunately, although they thought they were doing the right thing, I had no idea about access when I started, but I saw what was needed by the many hundreds of people with various disabilities I took on holiday. I would talk to hotels to see if they could make things better, and explain they would also be able to take more money because they had this facility. The difference was I was not in a wheelchair, but knew what they wanted. Unfortunately, from what I saw, the wheelchair user designed the room for themselves, which was not the way to do it.

There were many business people I met who saw the potential for change, and by changing, were not only able to serve disabled people, but of course make money at the same time. There were many people who I met that said they would feel a bit put-off by taking money from disabled people. I used to tell them that this wasn't the way to think, as it is the world we live in.

CHAPTER 8

THE NEED FOR ACCESSIBLE TRANSPORT

By now, you are all aware how I started in the accessible transport business. In my case, it was a business opportunity, which then went on to open other related business from the transport. to schools, holidays and working with the NHS There is an even bigger need for this now, as due to our population living longer, as we get older we will need more access. I see this a lot as older people on coach holidays have sometimes real problems getting off and on coaches. I have asked some of the operators have they not thought of having a lift on the side of the coach, as this will make it easier for the clients. It will in the end stop them coming as they find it harder and harder to get on and off. Some of the replies I have had sometimes surprises me. One told me they didn't want to go down that way, as they did not want to handle wheelchairs. They would however take people that just needed access getting on and off of the coach. The reason why they did not want wheelchairs was they would then need accessible rooms in the hotels they used, which was not going to happen for many years if at all. Also, all of the excursions would also have to be accessible for wheelchairs, and they did not want to go down this line.

Taking a step back, I can understand this. You have a product that works, and has done so for many years. As your clientele get older, they are finding it harder to get on and off of the coach. You put a lift on the coach to make it easier to board, other clients see the lift and immediately think you will be taking wheelchairs on future tours so you decide you won't be going again, as this isn't really for you. It is of course the choice of all clients to choose who they wish to go with on any escorted holiday, and what is not so normal now will be in the future, but it has to start somewhere sometime.

Only going back to 1980, I was the only company then operating accessible coaches and mini buses. As I have stated, we were always busy because we had found the gap in the market then, and as others recognize this, the more came into the market keeping the costs down. Accessible transport however goes a stage further as all can use it. So in the end, all passenger transport will be accessible as it adapts not only to the market now, but to the future aging market.

I remember going to a hotel promotion in the early 1980s where a hotel chain from Europe were showing how they had made their new hotel accessible to wheelchairs. This was quite something, and it was good to see how the hotel trade was responding. They showed us a film showing the outside of the hotel, and the access inside as well as the rooms. By the end of the presentation, the hotel company had gained many new friends as well as being praised for their achievement. It came to my turn to speak so I started by saying how pleased I was that they were taking notice, but that access only works when there is accessible transport as this would always be the key. I noticed the hotel was on top of a hill, so I asked if they knew of any accessible transport coach company or taxis, and they didn't. I said that in the years I had been working in this business, you had to look at three things to make it work. Accommodation, sea or air transport, and the most important accessible ground transportation because without the ground element, you can't get to the others.

Over the years, I have spent a lot of my time explaining that accessible transport is the key, and is so important. It is also the key even if there were no disability; as people get older, they find it harder to access buses and coaches, but do not count themselves as disabled.

I was so pleased when the law was passed to make all London cabs wheelchair accessible. This really was putting the UK in the lead. Over the years, it has been a great boon for disabled people coming to London from other parts over the UK as well as overseas. When running tours and arriving back at Heathrow, it is great to see wheelchair users from overseas being able to get in any black cab for hire. Of course, it isn't just black cabs, but many private hire vehicles are also becoming accessible. Once again creating commercial competition. We now need to see this at all the other airports in the UK, which is gradually happening; and for me, a great thing to see. Of course, as the accessible transport has grown, we have seen the growth in accessible hotels, and many of our public buildings including even older buildings. We run history tours all over the UK, and of course there are some buildings, which aren't accessible; but even though some are over seven hundred years old, we can still manage to go around them. Unfortunately, many people may never see the amount of access planning that is undertaken on many things, especially history where unique building cannot be altered; and yet, there are ways of making them accessible.

The amount of accessible vehicles in the UK keeps growing, and when we were asked to provide an ambulance service for an NHS hospital, trust it was good to be involved in the design of access in Patient Transport Services. My experience from my first accessible school bus, then holiday coaches, certainly helped in what was needed. As when I started providing holidays, I had underestimated just how much accessible transport there was in the UK.

This happened when the then Spastics Society (Scope) had to cancel their holiday programme, which Bill and I had set up for them even though they had bookings on them. The brochure had been sent out to the then sixty-four centres that made up the society at the time. We took over the programme, and used a society property in London as our departure point. The society transported the clients from their homes all over Britain in their own accessible vehicles to that point. The holidays were a success that year, and I had told Bill that next year, we would offer holidays to all disabilities not just CP.

It was not until I was many months into the planning when the subject of transport to and from London comes about, as of course, we knew how the CP clients would get to the pick-up point by using their own accessible transport as before; but now, this was being opened up to all disabilities where would the transport come from. How would they get to the pick-up point? It was then that I found out that all wheelchair users who travelled on a train had to go in the guards' van. When I was told this, I really did think it was a joke, but they were very serious about it. I thought we have sent a man to the moon, and yet we use the guards' van on a train to transport a wheelchair user!

When the new brochure was printed, I put in a section on how to get to the pick-up point; and if there was a problem with transport, to contact us, and we could see if we could help. At the time, I did have about thirty accessible smaller vehicles used to take children to school, and other services; and as many of the holidays departed and arrived back at a weekend, this worked in well with our transport. Over the next couple of years, I also built up a growing list of accessible taxis and private hire vehicles, and started using these companies. I also thought I would try including transport as an inclusive cost one year, but unfortunately, it didn't work out how I wanted. To make it economical, it meant that we had to get as many people on the vehicle as possible, which meant that sometimes, the first person on board could be on the vehicle for quite some time. Although it was a great improvement, as in a few years from now, transport or holidays with accessible transport will be included. At least things were going in the right direction.

Over the past thirty odd years, it is the improvement in transport, which has made accessible holidays more affordable. It has also meant that it has become easier to offer fully inclusive tours (FIT) holidays where people can look at a brochure (or go on- line) to see accessible hotels worldwide knowing they can go on their own, and not in escorted groups. Also, now there are growing amounts of accessible excursions due to the change in transport attitudes. Also, as we keep saying the travel industry is looking at the number of people who need access, and the new emerging market of older people, who need it as well. The changes are happening now and accessible travel will become mainstream. Sure there will always be room for specialist agencies dealing with disabled people in very specialised fields, like there is now with other markets, but there will soon be many more agencies dealing in both markets. This will have great advantages in both knowledge and costs, as the access will just be an add-on to the knowledge the agent already has in that part of the world. More and more travel organizations will make access an important part of their agency where they can mix it in with their itineraries so they don't even have to think about it in the future. I once suggested this to a well-known travel Agency who said that they had no intention of looking at the disabled travel market, as it was too time consuming, there were so many things to check, and it was too much in the public eye. I have since spoken to the same person who has now very much changed his mind.

CHAPTER 9

When I first got involved in accessible transport and holidays, what I found quite amazing was the sense of humour, which comes across from many people in which I sometimes thought was a serious situation at that time. Also, how they dealt with some silly comments from the general public. When I got to know disabled people, the comments from the public did sound a bit silly, but of course, I can see the other point of view as well because it was not until I began to know them I would have said the same things. The classic of course is when you are pushing someone, and you could be at a crossing or somewhere where you have stopped walking, and the person next to you asks you how the person in the wheelchair is. Of course, the classic answer is why don't you ask them until that is they come across someone with a terrible speech impediment, and feel embarrassed that they can't understand them.

Over the many years, I was involved in the running of escorted holidays for disabled people. I took people with many types of disability including people with terrible speech impediments, and I was taught by a professional that when listening to them, do not look at their mouths as you always tend to lip read—and worse—still try to finish of their words, which nine times out of ten is never what you think they are saying and is very frustrating for them. Also, if you have never pushed anyone in a wheelchair, there are many things you should be aware of. Being one of the first commercial operators running holidays for wheelchairs users showed me the problems of just transporting them in vehicles. How do you secure them, which way do they face— sideways, forward or backward. I learned on a coach that a wheelchair user would more than not be with their companion, spouse, or just friend, and would like to be by the side of them so they could talk and enjoy each other's company.

The first coach where we were allowed to keep clients in their wheelchairs was designed so that all of the wheelchairs were at the back of the coach behind all of the passengers who would be looking forward. This of course was not what I wanted for our passengers. They should be allowed to sit next to their partner even though they were in a wheelchair. After many meetings with Department of Transport, we started to look at seating on the nearside of the coach by removing seats, and using the tracking to hold the wheelchair. At the time, coach drivers were not trained in how to handle wheelchair passengers, especially those who didn't get out of their wheelchairs travelling in them on the coach. This alone allowed so many more disabled passengers to travel in some comfort like anyone else.

Taking on new coach drivers was a task that at the time only I could do, as I would train them in how to use all the facilities on the coach. So it would start with the usual interview, and the checking of their documents, then I would explain the type of work that we did. I must say there were many who didn't want to continue when they found out what the job entailed, as coach driving in the eighties took in holidays touring, and day trips, which they knew they would get tips. They were unsure about disabled people, and of course the extra work they would have to do. When I had selected a new potential driver, I would go out with them to show them how to use the equipment on the coach. Also, I would ask them not to push anyone in their wheelchair until I had shown them how to do this. Many would turn around and say, 'What is there to know? You just push!'

I said, 'Is that what you think?'

I would use one of our spare wheelchairs, and ask them to sit in it, but they had no use of their arms, hands, and legs. I would then push them onto the lift on the coach hitting the side of the chair. Their immediate reaction was to hold the sides of the chair for stability, and I reminded them they could not do that. I would then take them up on the lift where once again they would use their hands to steady themselves. I said no, you can't move. We would then go for a walk along the pavement where there were some drop kerbs to cross the road. I would find a drop where we would cross the road, but believe it or not, there was not one on the other side, and this at the time was very common. The driver of course did not notice this until we were halfway across where he put his feet to the floor. I said, 'You see what I mean about knowing how to push someone in their chair?'

So I put my foot on the back of the chair to tip him back to get on the pavement the other end. I would continue to do this training until I gave the job to my new manager. There were other problems operating in this new field, which was the fact that apart from us, no one trained drivers. So when we were a driver down through sickness, holidays ECT we could not go to a driver agency as they would not know how to operate the vehicle. This caused a few problems over the years, but got better when we trained some from the agency.

There was one strange factor, which I have never got to the bottom of, and that is driver's tips. I had been coach driving for many years, and whether it was a day trip or a holiday, you nearly always received a tip (depending on your attitude and helpfulness) at the end of the hire. When you had a coach with wheelchairs and slow walkers, you got very little—sometimes, if anything at all—and if the driver had been on a seven-day tour with a disabled group, the amount of extra work they had to do was far more than an able bodied group. This seemed to put off some drivers, as of course many needed their tips. What they couldn't understand was that they knew that the holidays we provided were not subsidised by charities, and that the clients had paid for themselves; and on many occasions, for their helper as well so they knew they had money.

Many times I was asked this question by different drivers, and when I was first asked, I really didn't know how to answer them. The reason being, I have always said that disabled people are the same as us, and just need the access so they can enjoy the same things as us; but of course, that reasoning doesn't work when it comes to

the coach driver's tips. So the only way to find out was to ask some of the clients who had been with me on previous holidays. Many had just not given it a thought, as of course many had not been able to go on coaches before. It was just as simple as that, or so I thought. Yes, for many, it was their first time on coach trips, but some of the carers told me that they knew of many that did not give tips as they were disabled and thought they never had to. I will leave it at that, as one could say. I have come across able-bodied people who did not give tips to coach drivers.

As time goes by, there will—and are already are—more accessible coaches, buses, taxis, etc., to enable more people to travel. It is changing for the better every year, as it is realized that the transport is the answer to improved access generally. I have always said that accessible coaches will have an advantage on standard coaches, as they are able to service both markets. I also helped with coach access in Hungary, Israel, and New Zealand, and also in the US. I also gave one of our first access coaches to Malta when we upgraded, and used it for many groups in Malta. It was a great feeling of satisfaction to see this happening in these different countries, as I thought it would be a start for all coaches and buses becoming accessible, and I am sure this is the future one day it just seems to be taking longer than I thought.

As I have explained at the beginning of the book, commercial accessible transport was to me just a new market and opportunity; and as I got more involved, I could see that access branched into many other markets giving people opportunities to enjoy what the majority of the population would take for granted. The main one of course, Holidays and travel, and it is the people and their stories that are amazing. A lady with polio joined a few of our holidays, and I know she enjoyed them. Indeed, I become a friend of her and two others who came with us, and lived in the same accessible flats. On one holiday, we were in the bar after dinner when she told me a story that I found amazing, and still do to this day. It all started as she had a South African accent, and I asked her was she born there, as it was very strong. She looked at me and said, 'This story could be a three pinter.'

'Well, I couldn't wait.'

'In the war, my mother and father lived in the old Czechoslovakia, which was controlled by the Nazis. My father was in the resistance, and one day was arrested and interrogated by the Gestapo, then for some unknown reason was released. He said to my mother that he had to get out because they were sure to come back, but he could not take my mother with him. The resistance got him to England where he helped the authorities with his knowledge. In 1942, the Nazis arrested my mother, and took her to Auschwitz. She ended up working for an SS officer who was always drunk, and was in charge of the Red Cross Parcels, which of course were never given out. It was from these she was able to steal food and survive.'

When the war finished, her father came over to Poland to see if he could find her. He found out where she had been taken, and went to the Red Cross to see if they had any information. They told him that if she had been there since that time, there was no way she had survived and was surely dead. He left Poland and got a job with a company in South Africa where he accepted her death, especially what he had seen in the area around Auschwitz. A year went by, and her father was having lunch in the canteen at work when he got talking to someone who used to work for the Red Cross—who was now quite high up in the company. He told him what had happened to his wife, and how the Red Cross in Poland told him she would not have survived.

'He said to my father, "did you not stay and look further?" He said "no, and after what I had seen around the area, I believed them." Look, he said to my dad "Give me all of the info you can, as I still know lots of people around that area." Well,' she said. 'A few weeks later they had found her, and were sending her out to be with my dad. Hence, my South African accent.'

I was just amazed. I said to her, 'That would make a great film.'

She told me that her mother had lived a long life, and always said to her she was never ashamed. She told her lots of stories about what happened, and how she had stayed alive; and one day even though she used a wheelchair, she might go back to see where she had been and survived. After hearing this, you think that sometimes you have problems, well it certainly puts thing into perspective. Now that is where her story ended at the time, but it would have an even better ending, but that was not planned then.

A few years later, I had this idea to do Eastern Europe, as it was starting to open up. The wall had come down in '89 and it was now coming up to '99, which I thought would be a good gap. I also had my new millennium executive coach, which was fitted out from new. I went to the Polish tourist board to get some idea on how accessible the country was. Unfortunately, the information was sparse. Of course they had many other things to sort out, and disability at that time was lower down the list. I was talking to one person about Auschwitz, and was this open now. He told me he had a lot of interest in the death camp, but he was puzzled how you would advertise this. I said you should call it a day of remembrance, and he seemed quite pleased with that. From putting the itinerary together, and waiting for replies took a couple of months, then Marian and I started our dummy run over the next two weeks to put it all together operational wise. The first two cities, Amsterdam and Berlin, were fine for access in the Hotels. I also knew that the hotel in Austria and Budapest was fine, as we had used these a few times. My main concern was the access in the hotels in Krakow and Prague, which on inspection, were fine. Auschwitz was a place that you did not expect to be accessible, but on the whole, it was with some help from my team.

The millennium had arrived, and it was the year 2000. As we all know, the computers did not die! The brochure was about to be sent out, and in it was the new central Europe holiday. I had spoken to many regular clients who were very interested, as of course for many years, that part of Europe was basically closed. I also spoke to Lillian who said she would definitely be booking, and to make sure I saved her a space. The tour filled up very quickly with most of the clients having been with us before. I would like to have repeated the holiday again that year, but decided to put it in the following year during the same time period; and this once again filled. This time with more new clients.

The day dawned, we were loading the coach for our Central Europe tour, and we're soon making our way to board the ferry to the Hook of Holland; and from there, to our hotel in Amsterdam. Over dinner, we were talking about how different it would be, and an experience as we travelled through Poland, Slovakia, and Hungry. It was very exciting for our clients, as none had ever been there before. I waited until they had finished their dinner to explain about the comfort stops between the hotels or excursions. The reason being that where there were service areas, there was no accessible toilets unlike the service areas on our motorways. So I suggested that the easiest way around this was that anyone who didn't need an access toilet could use the facilities in the services, and anyone who needed access could use the toilet on the coach, which was more than accessible. Everyone on the tour loved our new millennium coach, as it had all things needed to make the journey comfortable. It even had a camera, which would be aimed at the courier/guide who could sign and talk when we had a deaf or hard of hearing group on board. This is another thing I learned that disability is not just wheelchair users who you can see, there are deaf and blind people who need a different kind of access.

We were loading the coach outside the hotel in Krakow for our excursion to Auschwitz. Our guide worked in the hotel, and was the same person who had taken Marian and me there when we were on research. I looked in the coach and could not see Lillian, and she was not outside either. I went inside the hotel, and she was sitting at the breakfast table drinking a coffee. I said, 'Come on, we will be off shortly.'

She looked up at me with just a little tear in her eye. 'I don't think I can do this,' she said.

I took her hand and said, 'You can't come all this way and not go. What would your Mum say?' I squeezed her hand and said, 'Come on.'

Our first stop would be Auschwitz 1 we then crossed to Auschwitz 2. This is the one most people see on films where the train would enter under the arch. We arrived at Auschwitz 1, and the guide went inside to collect our tickets. We all got off the coach to gather outside to hear a talk from the guide. Once he had finished, we started to walk to the very famous gate. Lillian asked me if I would go round with her, which I did.

As we were going round, her face brightened up and she would say, 'Mum said that was here.' By the time we had finished, she had really got something from the tour.

That evening after dinner, we were all sitting around in the bar (nothing unusual there) when one of my team came over and said, 'Lillian would like to see you, and she wants to buy you a drink, which I am getting.'

I went over, and she got hold of my hand and said, 'On behalf of mum and me, we want to thank you because without you, your fabulous coach, and your ideas, I could not have done this tour.' I then had a tear in my eye, and if anyone ever asked why I do this job, it is because there is something more than money and that was it.

There are other times when you wonder why you are doing this job. This goes back to the early 1980s when I thought it would be a good idea to fly clients to Switzerland. Because there was no accessible coach, there I would send ours over empty where it could pick us up from the airport, and do the seven-day tour, then go back empty to the UK. I wanted to do this as the money it cost for two overnight stops would make the holiday about the same price, without the clients getting tired.

A friend I knew at the time run a well-known travel agency in London who specialized in flight costs, and knew people in the UK that worked for Swiss Air. He introduced me to one of their senior salesman, as I would need to use their special services. As this was going to be a holiday many months away, and indeed I was not that sure it would sell. I still needed the information for planning purposes. My discussions with the Swiss Air rep informed me that Switzerland at that time did not let empty coaches enter the country to be used there, as it would take away the business from Swiss coach operators. That I could understand, and if they could find me an accessible coach then I would use that. Of course, we all knew there wasn't one, so I would write to the Swiss embassy here in the UK to explain the situation so they were aware.

The holiday was arranged, and published in our brochure. The take up was excellent. Over the next few months, we got the air tickets and arranged the excursions, which of course we had done before. We would fly out on the Monday so I sent the coach out on the Friday with two drivers, so they could arrive late on Saturday giving them all of Sunday to rest up to pick us up on the Monday. Then the second coach driver would fly back as he would be needed in the UK. As planned, the coach left the UK for the ferry to France then to head for Basel where they would cross the border into Switzerland.

I was enjoying a nice doze when the phone woke me Saturday night. The person asked for Mr Reynolds. I confirmed he was speaking to me, and he told me his name, and that he was from the foreign office. I was now very confused, and thought he had the wrong number. He said that my coach was at the Swiss border, and they wanted it to return to France as they had refused its entry. He also said as an operator, I should have known this, and could I telephone my driver and tell him to go back. I then told him the history of the coach and how I had sent the embassy in London a letter explaining the coach was accessible for wheelchairs and as they did not have one we were exempt and they agreed. He asked if

I could fax him a copy, I said the letter was in my office, but could do it the next day. He said he would call them back, and explain it to the people at their office who would inform the border. In the end, it was agreed they would let the coach in, provided the driver went to one of their offices in Zurich where they might give him a permission letter for the length of stay. I thought this is a good start to the holiday because when I land with the group at 2.00 p.m., it will not be certain I will have my coach. I spoke to the driver when he arrived at the Swiss hotel in the early hours, and he told me he told them he was not going to move only into Switzerland. I said to see the manager of the hotel in the morning, and ask him if he could help as I do know him. Sure enough, the driver rang me on Sunday to say that the manager knew where the office was, and was going to go with him.

Monday arrived, and we were coming into land at Zurich. We went off the aircraft, and went through to passport control and then luggage. I looked outside, and gave a great sigh as I saw the coach. The driver came over, and had the letter. The other driver had checked in, and would soon be on his way back to London. I had aged another ten years! The holiday was a great success, and of course the clients never knew (until now)

It was a good job I was told by the Swiss Air person about empty coaches entering Switzerland at the time because this was once again all new territory, and had to be coped with. There were also situations on the holidays that I hadn't thought of, which clients asked if I could help them. One request was from a client who was a wheelchair user, and used an electronic writing board to speak. He would then sometimes shout or put his thumbs up to let me know he had understood. I knew he liked the girls, which is fine. Just because you are disabled, in my view, it shouldn't matter. I would go into his room in the mornings, and he would be on the balcony looking at the women staff arriving at the hotel. Nothing wrong in that, and sometimes, I would pull up a chair and join him making him laugh at some of my comments. He must have felt comfortable in my company, as using his board, asked me if I could take him to the lap dancing club in the town where he could be in the company of a young lady for the evening. I was a bit taken aback thinking I would have to explain to her how he communicates. I told him he would have to pay her, and buy all the drinks. He seemed happy with this arrangement. The following evening, we arrived at the lap dancing club which had a flight of stairs but luckily two burly bouncers carried him down, a young lady approached us and sat next to him but instead of talking to him she was complaining that the pole was too slippery eventually it was her turn to dance which was rather erotic when she returned she sat on his lap for a while and had a few drinks he had a smile on his face for the rest of the holiday.

I would say to our clients, the more you travel, the more access will change until one day it will just happen. Indeed, when I speak to a wheelchair user who is under twenty, they find it difficult to understand how people coped then. I have always put it to suppliers that more access will create more money because it creates more users. This I would pass onto overseas agents that were starting to appear as they could see a business opening.

I have one such agent in South Africa who contacted me after I did a video link where people asked me questions about why and how I did things in my business; and if I were to bring clients to South Africa, could I advise them on what would be needed. There was one agent who I got know, and over the years, sent many groups to. We spent a lot of time finding a coach that's big enough to take our groups, and this was based in Johannesburg;and we had to pay for it to come down to Cape Town—not a short distance. She sent me some photographs, and it looked okay. So we worked out a cost, and put it in our brochure. She corresponded with me about the rest of the tour, and what she had arranged at different places. She telephoned one day, very excited to let me know that she was involved with seven baby cheetahs who had been hand-reared, and she would like some of the wheelchair clients to stroke them as they might find this a great adventure. I said my clients come with me for an adventure, and do things they might not do on their own. I said, 'Are you sure they would be safe?'

'Oh, yes,' she said.

The day dawned when we were at the adventure park to be introduced to the cheetahs I had already asked my wheelchair users if they wanted to stroke the cheetahs, and they had all agreed and were very eager to do this. The chairs were all in a line across the path when the handlers each with a cheetah on a lead came up to the wheelchair that was in front of them. There were six wheelchairs and seven cheetahs, and as they came up to the wheelchair, the clients put out their hands to stroke them. The seventh one waited by the side of one of the chairs. Both the clients and the cheetahs thoroughly enjoyed this. Mike who had been with me on many holidays was really laughing loud when the seventh cheetah, who must have thought he was missing out, decided to go around the back of his chair, and jumped up putting his claws on his shoulders. A great sense of panic went round the park, and of course me. Mike was very calm, and just sat still in his chair. The handler took the cheetah away from the front of Mike. The handler of the other at his back was trying to get his paws off his shoulders. She did this after a minute or so, which seemed like hours to me, and poor Mike's shirt had been ripped, and he had scratch marks on his shoulders. They then took Mike into the little clinic as they had to make sure he was okay. He emerged about twenty minutes later with a brand new shirt telling his story to all around him. In the bar later the comment was made that the cheetah thought Mike was a meal on wheels

As you can imagine, my agent was very upset about the incident, as she was thinking the worst—if Mike had been attacked. I said to her we make decisions in good faith weighing up any risks. Mike didn't get hurt, and he is okay, and many others had a great time with the cheetahs. After all, you could have had no idea he would jump up at the back of the wheelchair. Maybe if you do this again, and if I were you I would, it would be to only take the amount of cheetahs to the amount of wheelchairs. That seemed to cheer her up a bit, and we drove on to our next attraction.

Pam was—and still is—a fantastic agent whose training as a nurse gives her an advantage. When I was tour managing with a group in South Africa, Pam would ask many questions on how to make things accessible, and would explain how easy it is sometimes to do this and at a little cost. Once again, I would make it clear to her, and many of my agents that access starts with transport. At the time, there was very little accessible transport in South Africa. Apart from the coach we would use, that was all. Pam decided to purchase her own smaller accessible vehicle, and go for smaller groups. She has done very well with groups from Europe and the US.

What happened to Pam is something that happens when you don't expect it. Running tours and planning can go wrong in the most unusual ways. I remember running a tour in Devon, and one of the excursions was to the Eden Project. The night before, I was having dinner with the group, and on my table was a new lady client who used a wheelchair for distance, but also used it to walk as well. So we would supply her with a pusher who we had got to know over the years and we would meet at the Projec. She told me that she was looking forward to the next day, and the ride to the Project as she had heard so much about it. I told her that I had been there many times, and she would find it fascinating.

The next day dawned, and I made my way to the dining room for breakfast. Most of the group was there so I got some breakfast, and sat on the same table as I was on yesterday with the same people. I said to the lady not long now, and we will be at the Eden Project. Everyone was pleased, and looking forward to it. I gave them the time for loading before going to the other tables to inform them. The lady I was talking to the night before came over to me, and asked the name of the lady that was going to push her around the Project. I told her and said, 'I am sure you will both get on very well together.'

She said she was going to her room for a little rest before coming down to the coach. I asked her if she wanted a call, and she said no.

I finished my breakfast, and went to my room to get my briefcase with the tickets and other docs. I then went to the coach where the driver was sorting out the clamps, and straps for the wheelchairs. My helpers would load the coach with the driver, and by now had got a good system working. I would also help before doing the all- important count before leaving. I helped with a couple of clients, and started the count. I got halfway through when someone asked me something; and I forgot where I was, and had to start again. It was here that caused the problem, as I must have counted the driver as a client.

We arrived at the project and were unloading when the pusher for the lady arrived, and that is when I found out she was not on the coach. My heart sunk, and began to pump harder. This was the excursion she had been waiting for. She would go mad, and quite rightly so. I said to Denis did he not know she wasn't on board, he said no. I rang the hotel who told me she was not around. I asked them if they could go to her room, as I thought something might have happened to her. They then said that she had been in bed, and had not woken up, and they would look after her the rest of the day. Although relieved, I just felt so sorry for her, and was annoyed with myself for not ringing her room before we started loading. That's how you have to be so careful when making a count. It really is easy to make a mistake, especially when you have people who are kneeling securing wheelchairs. To this day, it never happened again.

When I got back I apologized to the lady, and she said she wished she had taken me up on my offer to call her as she just went into a deep sleep for no reason. You would think that was bad enough the next day was a short excursion to Teignmouth, so I thought I would push the lady to the shops, and then take her for a nice lunch. As we were going through the pedestrian part of the town, I could see some of our group by the ice cream shop. I asked her if she would like one, and she said she would. Maureen, one of my helpers, and Denis were there with their clients, and they had got very large ninety-nine cornets with the chocolate attached in the ice cream. I got my lady one as well, and thought I would have a cigarette. I walked away from them so the smoke did not affect them. Then there was this loud shout from Maureen, as she was trying to get some sea gulls away from the client's ice creams. I too rushed over, and this gull had got my ladies ice cream in his beak when another one come along, and tried to get it from the other gull. My lady got pecked as they stole her ice cream, and flew off with it. We took her to a doctor to be checked out, and didn't have our lunch either. So be careful with ice cream, seagulls, and wheelchairs.

Every country has something that tourist will want to see. I remember going to Paris where I met a person who was himself disabled, and wanted to start up a touring company for wheelchair users. I said I had many customers who have expressed a wish to holiday in France, and he had the same for the UK so we both thought let's get this organized. I spent a few days with him in Paris looking around at the access at the venues, and how we could make them more accessible where needed. One struck me as somewhere many UK tourists would like to see, and that was Napoleon's Tomb, due to its history. People who have been there before will know that there are enormous amount of steps to get inside. I said to the agent, 'What a shame as this would be really good to visit, but for wheelchairs, this was not going to happen.'

A year later, we were running a week based in Paris with fifteen wheelchairs, total thirty-six pax, our agent had got over many problems, and made it possible for us to visit many attractions including the palace of Versailles where he had got permission for us to stay in our coach, and were escorted by the police from the coach park to the top. Without this, it would have been very difficult to push wheelchairs uphill on a cobbled road, and after the visit we would load the coach and be escorted down. Whilst we were loading the coach, many people were watching, and these were tourist from around the world. A British coach making this holiday accessible to wheelchair users, I was so pleased because it all started from Social Services back in the UK not having the transport for the new school; and of course, the lady in-charge having the faith in me providing it— funny how things turned out.

I will always have faith in my French agent, as what happened next on the tour was just unbelievable, and would never happen now. We were making our way back to Paris from Versailles when he said our next stop would be Napoleon's Tomb. I looked at him, and he smiled. I said, 'How could you have done this?'

He said, 'Just wait and see.'

As we pulled into the parking area, I could see all these sheets of wood put over the steps, and about twenty police officers waiting. As we unloaded the coach, they took the wheelchair, and between two, or sometimes three, officers pushed them to the top. I just could not believe what I was seeing it was just amazing. I said to my agent, 'How the hell did you manage this?'

He laughed and said, 'Could you do this in England?'

I didn't say no, but didn't say yes either. To see all this happening worldwide was truly something to see, and how far could we take this. Over the years, much further in some cases, but there seems to be a stop to total integration; and I find that hard to understand why.

There are many more specialist access operators worldwide than ever before. All mainstream buses are accessible, and many more access hotels; and yet, it still isn't joined up. My view is that as things become more mainstream, most travel agents should be able to give information, and the amount of specialist agents would decrease. This has not yet happened because maybe mainstream want to leave the disabled market to the specialist organizations. Also, it has come to light that in a survey carried out in the UK, eighty-five per cent of shops on the high street are not very accessible. That could mean the width of aisles, the lack of toilets just silly things that in many cases could be avoided, especially if it was a newish building. I have also contacted mainstream travel agents, and told them the holiday I was interested in, and that one of the passengers was a wheelchair user and could arrangements be made. Unfortunately, there would be no answer for at least a week or so then not an answer to all of the questions. After seeing and being part of the great changes being made in access to me, it seems to have slowed down just when it will be needed for the growing amount of older people needing access. It's as though a big halt sign has been erected, and when disabled people do try to make bookings, people seem to want to know their life history. I don't know why this is, but what I do know is that travel for disabled people must continue to grow until it just becomes the norm. I would now like to give you my view and ideas on how transport should progress in the UK, and of course, worldwide.

Accessible transport is of course a new concept, as I didn't get any accessible vehicles until the 1970s, so there has been a great move forward since then—both in the public and private sectors. The UK has done a lot to improve access across the country. There is a lot more awareness here than there was in the early 1980s. This is because at last, many transport companies can see that having accessible vehicles will give them access to another market. Indeed, London taxis are all accessible. Also, as explained earlier, access is not just for wheelchair users, it is for prams and pushchairs making it easier for parents pushing these around shops etc. More importantly, is the older market. This is growing at a fast rate, and it means access will be easier for them without having to climb steps. That puts a different angle on all forms of travel, which mean more people travelling, and these people will not all be from the UK because if older people from overseas can see it is easy to get around, they will come here.

Accessible transport also has an effect on cruises, as although many of the cruise ships I have taken clients on have great facilities. They seem to have forgotten that wheelchair users will be stuck on the ship unless they are able to get on the coaches used for shore excursions. When we operate escorted cruises, we find out if there are access vehicles on any of the shore excursions; and although this is getting better, there are still a lot of places where this does not happen. Once again, this is just another case to show how without ground transport you have this problem. My ultimate aim would be to see all vehicles accessible, and this would have a great effect on all business as it will create more customers. It would free the many millions worldwide who stay at home, and of course, once again this number will carry on increasing with people getting older.

Over the many years, I got involved with access in hotels, and could see that there was a cost to converting rooms in the early days. Of course, someone would have to pay for this. However, when it comes to building new hotels, that was a different matter. I was very impressed with the Princess trust who I had got involved with over time, as they had a section called the Hotel Forum where they listened to ideas, and come up with the idea of Individual all. This was where hotel rooms were all accessible using grab rails that were put in by the toilet, and bed to the height where the client wants. Also the bathroom was accessible with a roll in shower, and when the client left the hotel, the rails were taken out, and the room could be used by anyone. They also had hearing aid loops for people with hearing problems. This was a clever system, as it kept the costs down, and it did what it was called individual all because any person with any disability is just that individual unique.

This is so true when it comes to the deaf and hard of hearing, as there is no visual disability. You only find out when you try to communicate. Over the years, I spoke to many deaf and hard of hearing people who told me that when it comes to coach travel, it would be so much better that if they had a signing guide that could sign to a camera, so that they could see them on the screens and understand what was being said. Also, there were the hard of hearing with a T on their hearing aid, and if the coach had that in the sound system, it would make the whole journey so much better. The cost of doing this was not very much at all. Also, you could play videos with subtitles. I designed a new coach in 1996 with the help of Van Hool in Belgium, and wanted a sound system like an aircraft where there were eight channels to choose from. This would mean that passengers could choose from radio, CD, and video channels.

So there was no noise in the coach so people could still have conversations. Also, we fitted a T-loop so anyone with a hearing aid could also choose. This coach was well ahead of its time, and was also featured on the BBC See Hear programme. The coach could take people in their wheelchairs, and of course people who found it difficult to get upstairs. Now, the deaf and hard of hearing, so surely this is the way it should be in the future. That was operational in 1997, and to this day, there is not another one like it. It is not the cost, as you are able to take passengers that standard coaches cannot. Operators should be encouraged to see that this is the future, and if you don't do it, others will get the business. Legislation has its place, but in the end business will see the benefits eventually!

CHAPTER 10

AND FINALLY

Over the many years I have been involved in this business, many people—mostly clients—used to say to me, 'You should write a book about your experiences with accessible transport and holidays, as it is very rare that someone is involved all be it by accident in such an interesting business from its start.' Of course, I never looked at it like this; but over the years, I began to realize that through my experience, I was seeing things just in transport other operators were not. This also applied to hotels, airports, and cruise lines. I also see things through business' eyes, and look at the long-term profit, so I am able to talk to suppliers to show them what is possible, which they understand. I have also shown some cruise companies where to look for accessible coaches or smaller vehicles, as I have had to do when running escorted cruises worldwide. Nevertheless, I still see many cruise companies where they can't offer shore excursions to wheelchair users even though they provide sometimes over thirty coaches on shore excursions with many of those coaches from one operator. Would it not be easy just to ask that coach operator to provide one of the thirty coaches that is accessible? I am sure the company would do this if they thought they would lose work from the cruise company. This is a way to increase their passenger loadings with not just wheelchair users. It sometimes is a problem to get this point over to business, and government decision makers, as many times they just can't see this because so many people think access just means wheelchairs—and of course it does not. My involvement with the deaf and hard of hearing made me realize how they tend to be ignored, not intentionally it mainly is that you cannot see their disability.

For many years, all the tours I ran were for escorted groups where we also supplied any assistance, which was asked for by the client. These holidays are always more expensive because there is only a limited amount of accessible rooms in any hotel, which will limit the amount of wheelchair clients you are able to take; and of course, means the costs are shared by fewer people. It has always been my intention to run escorted holidays where it was a mixture of people, but unfortunately, as I have said, this is very difficult to achieve. I hope it is just a matter of time for this to happen, but I have yet to see this in the standard holiday brochures—maybe I am just impatient.

People's perceptions never cease to amaze me, as when I started with coach holidays, I wanted to use good quality hotels, which I did. I always remember one couple in one of the hotels in the UK, saying to each other, 'how can these disabled people afford to come to hotels like this?' I would have thought this was way out of their reach. I didn't say anything at the time, but was ashamed of their attitude, and over the years was determined to change this outlook some people had. I also would get questioned by some hotel managers when asking about a holiday booking if I was sure this hotel would be suitable. I would say it would be better if it had more access rooms, but the ones you have are fine then the penny would drop, it really was would they fit in here. This wasn't just in the UK, but also many places in mainland Europe. The USA was better at that time, especially Disneyworld, and the new theme parks being built. Nevertheless, there were still many other up market hotels that had an excuse why they couldn't take my clients. That in the end would be a great misjudgement thinking all disabled people had no money. Unfortunately, things sometimes go against disabled people when things are taken to far the other way. I have overheard many people at supermarkets complaining about how many disabled parking bays there were, and especially in the rain, when they have to park to them a long way, away from the store due to the empty disabled bays. 'There were far too many,' I hear them say. Sometimes on the surface, maybe they have a point.

So surely to please everybody cut down on some of the amount of disabled bays, and let anyone with a disabled badge park in two standard bays when the entire disabled bays are taken. Sometimes, just a bit of thought and experience can solve what sometimes seems to be a problem. We get this now when just recently a wheelchair passenger was waiting for a bus. When the bus arrived at the stop, there was a pram already in the space the wheelchair would take so the wheelchair could not get on. I find this strange as in 1980, I was invited to join the transport panel at the Department of Transport. Next year1981 was the international year for disabled people, and the department wanted to see how they could make buses accessible for wheelchairs. This was a long task, and before deregulation but now under the law, all buses must conform to take wheelchairs. They didn't alter buses to make them accessible for prams and buggies, as they were already travelling on the non- accessible buses. It is because of the wheelchair access it has improved the access for the other users, so surely wheelchair users should have priority. I know many people that might not agree with me, but that is my view, as I was part of the changes on the buses at the time.

The many years that have passed since I become involved in this business (yes, business) have been so interesting and productive, but sometimes frustrating when people cannot understand what you mean—and sometimes, they don't want to. This refers to everyone saying that the only way forward is total inclusion. I know, and so do many others that this is of course the way to go; but it takes time— and to some people—a change in attitude. There have been many times when I have advertised a day trip to different events in the local papers, which have been successful with able-bodied passengers; and when I put the same advert in saying that if you use a wheelchair or scooter, you are still able to come—as the coach has a lift—then only disabled people booked. If I hadn't done this myself, I would never have believed it. Also, whenever I tell people this, they find it hard to believe. So you can see integration is very hard to achieve, and it isn't through the lack of trying. When there are organizations involved it is another situation, as we have taken organizations away, which are a mixture of disability and able- bodied. This is usually when the organization is to do with the disabled person's occupation where an accident happened when they were doing their job at that time.

Running holidays like these are so different than other tours, as mainly, you tend to be in one location with excursions every other day so as to keep the travelling time down. Also, you are able to give people a choice whether they want to go or not as some might just prefer a more relaxing time, and I believe this is a choice they should always have. As these tend to be large groups, as many as 200 finding accommodation for approximately 25–35, wheelchairs can be a challenge if you don't want specialist hotels that just look after people with disabilities. I am finding more hotels having more access rooms now than they would have had a few years ago. Once again, I believe this is due to hoteliers becoming more aware of the ageing population.

To the subject of airports and airlines, as I have said, unfortunately this is something that is mostly out of their control due to the terrorist element involved. Nevertheless, over the many years I have been involved in using both airports and airlines, I have come across some undesirable practices. The worst was the practice of taking away a person's electric wheelchair at check in, and taking them to a place through passport control and security to be parked up until collected to be taken to the flight gate that of course was if they were remembered, as I have heard of passengers who were forgotten, and missed their flight. Also, it had been forgotten that the electric wheelchair was their independence, so they could choose which shops and cafes to go to. I had come across this many times, and said to the airlines, 'If you wish to take their electric chair, then you should put someone with them until they went to the gate.'

As you can imagine, there were many reason put up for this practice, but I am glad to say it has gotten better now. This could be something to do with the airport now in charge of the new PRM (people with reduced mobility) rather than the airlines, and this is EU wide.

The message on the importance of accessible transport is it seems still not getting out. As I noticed on a report on the television the other day, that although the Paralympics stadiums for the Olympic games next year are accessible, it is the infrastructure and again the transport, which is missing; and over the many years I have stated this is the first thing to look at. Surely when picking a country to hold the games, the transport should be looked at and introduced ready for the games. After all, anyone can use accessible transport where everyone gains, and which will make more money for the operator. Increase future tourism bring in money for the country.

I find it sometimes very strange when I see access symbols all over, as there were none when I started in this very interesting business. I have enjoyed the time I have spent on transport, and seeing it through its changes; and have now been out of this for a few years, but we still have the holiday company. Seeing how the changes have really made a difference, not only in people's lives, but how new business has come about because of it. I now spend most of my time putting together British history tours mainly for people overseas, and these tours are truly inclusive. I also like consulting with business and government agencies to show how access makes things better for all, and I have proved this over the many years. Just recently, I watched on the news about people's perception on disability, how there is something still stopping them getting fully engaged. Not all of course, and the sooner this number gets smaller, the sooner we will have full integration including holidays.

www.ingramcontent.com/pod-product-compliance
Lightning Source LLC
Chambersburg PA
CBHW071010120626
46546CB00003B/1028